Project Management
Interview Questions

Project Management
Interview Questions

by

Shivprasad Koirala

Sham Sheikh

BPB PUBLICATIONS

B-14, CONNAUGHT PLACE, NEW DELHI - 110 001

FIRST EDITION 2008

Copyright © 2008 BPB PUBLICATIONS, INDIA

ISBN 10 : 81-8333-257-9
ISBN 13 : 978-81-8333-257-6

LIMITS OF LIABILITY AND DISCLAIMER OF WARRANTY

Distributors:

COMPUTER BOOK CENTRE
12, Shrungar Shopping Centre, M.G. Road,
BANGALORE-560001 Ph: 25587923, 25584641

MICRO BOOKS
Shanti Niketan Building, 8, Camac Street,
KOLKATA-700017 Ph: 22826518/9

BUSINESS PROMOTION BUREAU
8/1, Ritchie Street, Mount Road,
CHENNAI-600002 Ph: 28410796, 28550491

BPB PUBLICATIONS
B-14, Connaught Place, NEW DELHI-110001
Ph: 23325760, 23723393, 23737742

BPB BOOK CENTRE
376, Old Lajpat Rai Market, DELHI-110006
PH: 23861747

MICRO MEDIA
Shop No. 5, Mahendra Chambers, 150 D.N. Rd,
Next to Capital Cinema V.T. (C.S.T.) Station,
MUMBAI-400001 Ph.: 22078296, 22078297

DECCAN AGENCIES
4-3-329, Bank Street,
HYDERABAD-500195 Ph: 24756400, 24756967

INFO TECH
G-2, Sidhartha Building, 96 Nehru Place,
NEW DELHI-110019
Ph: 26438245, 26415092, 26234208

INFO TECH
SHop No. 2, F-38, South Extension Part I,
NEW DELHI-110049
Ph: 24691288

Published by Manish Jain for BPB Publications, B-14, Connaught Place, New Delhi-110 001 and Printed by him at Akash Press New Delhi

What's in the CD

We have tried to pack some good goodies to help you in project management. Feel free to experiment and exploit the same.

- **Resume.doc** :- Simple resume template to kick start your resume from project management perspective. A detailed explanation is also given below in the resume preparation section for the same. We know that many can make better resumes than this; we have kept it simple to avoid confusion.
- **Interview Rating Sheet.xls** :- This is a simple excel sheet which will help you judge till what level you are ready for project management interviews. Just be truthful to yourself when you are using this excel sheet.
- **FunctionPoints(Accounting Application)** :- This excel sheet has a simple sample TPA estimation for white box testing.
- **Documents folder:** - This folder has some basic documents from SDLC point of view for a simple chat application. It has four important documents estimation document (using function points) , requirement document (Reliable Chat Application Version.doc) , technical document and test plan. This is only for reference purpose to get a feel of basic documentation in project.
- **COCOMO Software folder:** - You can learn how to estimate using COCOMO I, II and III. It's developed by COSTAR and pretty good tool to evaluate for project managers who are looking to estimate using LOC (Lines of Code).
- **HowtoPrepareSoftwareQuotations.pdf** :- One of my old books completely dedicated to software estimation.
- **Use Case Points Software:** - We have shipped two software's one is the enterprise architect and the other is an open source petalo. Feel free to evaluate them and see how use case points estimation can benefit you.
- **Function point Workbench:** - A cool estimation tool to see function point estimation in action.
- **Estimation Templates Folder:** - This is again cool collection of good estimation templates made for function points and use case points in Microsoft excel. For a detail understanding on how to use them please read the 'How To Prepare Software Quotation.pdf' for details.
- **MPMM:** - Method 123 Project Management Methodology tool to for project management. Feel free to use it to make WBS, Gantt chart and for practicing project planning.
- **smartdraw_11M_4EW24_setup:**- Good tool to draw fish bone diagram to do CAR analysis.

Features of the Book

- This book is best suited for team leads who want to jump in to the project management role and as well as for seniors who want to have a quick revision from project management interview perspective.
- It starts with basics of project management fundamentals like ROI, stake holders, MOU, SDLC, CAR, DAR, traceability matrix and then rises towards more sophisticated questions.
- Estimation is the most frequented section during project management interviews. A full chapter with 40 questions is dedicated to estimation. This chapter covers the most used estimation methodology like COCOMO, LOC , Function points and Use case points.
- Many project managers fall out when it comes to answer questions on schedule management. Full chapter on schedule management covering fundamentals like EST, LFT, EFT, LST, PERT, GANTT and Monte Carlo. We are sure by knowing these fundamentals you can not slip.
- This book does full justice by dedicating a complete chapter to costing. The costing chapter covers the most asked fundamentals like Earned value, planned value and Actual cost with some real examples.
- Small and sweet chapter on risk management which covers basics like DR and BCP.
- CMMI which has evolved as a very matured and standard process across IT industry is the biggest talk during project management interviews. Full blown chapter on CMMI covering maturity levels, staged and continuous representation, SCAMPI, PII and full details explanation of all CMMI KPA (Key Process Area).
- Six sigma is catching up very fast in the IT industry and also one of the most frequented section during project management interviews. Nice and sweet 20 pages document dedicated to six sigma.
- Agile and XP has caught lot of attention in the recent times. This book has dedicated a full 50 pages document to Agile, XP, SCRUM, FDD and LSD.
- The best part of the book is the CD in which we have provided standard templates and softwares by which you can gain a insight of project management tools.
- We have also provided a sample resume by which you can get a fair idea of how to prepare a resume from a project management job perspective.
- Project management Interview rating sheet which is provided with CD will help you to measure and rate yourself before going to interviews.

Acknowledgments

This book is dedicated to my kids, Sanjana and Simran, whose play-time has been stolen and given to the creation of this book. I am also thankful to my wife for constantly encouraging me, and also to BPB Publication that gave a newcomer like me a platform to perform. Last, but not the least, i would like to thank my mom and dad for constantly blessing me. I am indeed lucky to have my brother, Raju, who always keeps my momentum preserved. I am also grateful to Bhavnesh Asar who initially conceptualized the idea of this series of books on interview questions. And before I forget, thanks to Shaam for all the effort he has put in. It was his tiresome three months of continuous writing that made sure that we made it in time. Tons of thanks to my reviewers whose feedbacks were an essential tool that helped improve this book.

Shivprasad Koirala

The credit of being a part of this book goes to three persons: my mom, dad, and Mr Shivprased. I mentioned my mom and dad because of all that they did for me and the sacrifices that they made for me, and I mentioned Mr Shivprased because it was he who taught me how to share knowledge through books. I thank him from my bottom of my heart for giving me an role to play in the creation of this book. And above all, I thank the almighty Lord sitting above all of us for showing his presence, and showering his blessings and love in the form of these three persons. In case you want to get in touch with me, mail at ahteshamax@hotmail.com.

Sham Sheikh

About the Author

Shivprasad Koirala works in a multinational company and has extensive experience in the software industry. He is presently working presently as a project lead, and has, in the past, led projects in banking, travel, and financial sectors. But all in all, he is still a developer at heart working an 8-hour job. Writing is something that he does on the side because he loves writing. The author understands that nobody is perfect. He is, therefore, open to and welcomes any and all comments and criticisms, which can be mailed to shiv_koirala@yahoo.com. The author would like to reassure his readers that all bouquets and brickbats would be received with love and shall be treated with topmost priority.

The author understands that writing an interview question book is a big responsibility. He has tried to cover the maximum number of questions for each the topic in this book. But it is pretty much impossible to cover all questions that can probably be asked. So if any reader comes across any such questions during an interview, that reader is requested to mail it to shiv_koirala@yahoo.com .Who knows, that question can probably secure someone else's job!

Organizational Hierarchy

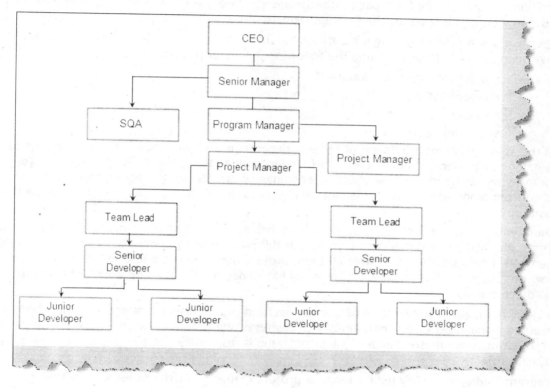

Figure: - IT company hierarchy

Note: *In small-scale and mid-scale software houses, chances are that they expect a PM to be very much technical. But in big software houses the situation is very much different, interview are conducted according to positions applied for.... Unless the interviewer changes the rule.*

Note: *There are many small and medium-sized software companies that do not follow the hierarchy ahown in the figure above, and have their own* **adhoc** *way of defining positions in the company.*

So why is the need of hierarchy in an interview? *"Interview is a contract between the employer and candidate to achieve specific goals."*

So, an employer is looking for a suitable candidate and a candidate is looking for a better career. Normally in interviews, the employer is very clear about what type of candidate he is looking for, but 90% of the time, the candidate is not clear about the positions he is looking for. How many times has it happened with you that you have given a whole interview and when you mention the position you are looking for... pat comes the answer, "we do not have any requirements for this position." So be clear about the position right from the start.

When we say a project manager's position it has lot of flavors attached. In IT companies we have seen project manager having the following flavors of positions.

- Project manager position itself.
- Program manager.
- Manager.
- Senior manager.

All the above positions are flavors of project managers means during interview they will be asked questions of project management. So first let's understand these flavors. Above figure 'IT Company hierarchy' shows how a software company is structured. Project manager questions are asked from team lead and above. So let's understand the hierarchy from team lead to the top IT position.

Team lead: - They are expected to do 80% technical and 20 % management. They mostly look after senior and junior developers. If you are at this position and you want to be a project manager then you should be able to answer all basic project management questions. From my point of view this stage is a crucial stage where a guy has to decide that does he want to be architect or a project manager.

Project manager:- They are expected to perform pure project management activities like resource management , estimation , day to day reporting to top management , metrication etc. A project manager mostly handles one project and is responsible for all good and bad pertaining to that project.

Program Manager: - They lead a team of project managers or the other way of saying is that they lead a group of projects. They have a bird eye view of what's happening on the project side. They are normally a point of contact for escalation issues for the project they are leading. They are also involved in interaction with end customer for contract renewal and customer escalation.

Senior manager: - They lead a complete geographical delivery unit. Mostly they are above program managers and one point of contact with the owner CEO or board of directors of the company. There are many fine versions of this position available like manager, Deliver head etc, but more or less the roles are same. One of the main responsibilities of senior manager is to ensure that projects follow SQA procedures and to ensure customer satisfaction. So normally SQA comes directly under senior managers in many companies.

Now depending on what you are looking at you should prepare yourself. The above hierarchy is a generalized one every company has his own tailored version, but more or less they fall in the same lines.

There are two important points which we wanted to discuss and you can face this problem when you are moving from one position to other.

The jumps from a team lead to Project manager

Normally team lead position is a decisive making point for any individual. In a team leads role you are normally doing two kinds of activities one is the technical and the other is project management. But moving next level from here you need to decide do you want to grow as a full fledged technical architecture or want to go completely as a project manager. If you are thinking of growing in terms of project manager you need to go deep in to the same. You need to sacrifice your so called technical love (if you have it) and dwell more in to people issues, metrication, process etc. A word of caution team leads try to show of more of technical capabilities during interview rather than management skills. So when jumping from this level be careful and try to control your technical love.

For small companies it always goes -1 level or same level

This is one more typical scenario where a person who is working in a small scale or mid Scale Company wants to jump to a next level in an international organization. It's really difficult that you are working as a team lead in a small organization and you get a project manager position in an international organization. I have seen rare success rate where teams lead of a smaller organization rises to a project manager level in a bigger organization through interview. In most cases we have always seen he has to go -1 his level or same level. That means he has to either join as a team lead or a -1 level below team lead (senior software engineer) but not to the next level. This is just a suggestion and not to demotivate you, if you are working in a smaller organization be ready for -1 or same level, on a longer run it can be fruitful.

Guidelines to a Good Resume

> **Note:** *First impression the last impression.*

> **Note:** *A sample resume is provided in the CD from project management perspective.*

Even before the interviewer meets you, he/she will first meet your resume. An interviewer looking at your resume is almost 20% of the interview happening without you knowing it. I was always bad guy at preparing resumes. Now that I am writing a series of book on interviews, I thought that I should devote a section to resumes. You can skip this part if you are confident about your resume. There is no hard and fast rule that you have to follow, but just see if the following points hold true for your resume.

- Use plain text when sending resumes through email. For instance, if you create your resume using Microsoft Word, what happens if the interviewer is using Linux? He will never be able to read your resume. And what if you create your resume in MS-Word 2000 and the interviewer has Word 97? Ouch!
- Always attach a covering letter to your application. It looks traditionally formal and is really impressive. Attach a covering letter even if you are sending your CV through email.

Given below is a check-list of what you should have in your resume:

- Start with an objective or summary, for example:

- o   Working as a project manager for more than 4 years. Did estimation independently using function points and COCOMO.
- o   Followed the industry's best practices, and adhered and implemented processes that enhanced the quality of technical delivery.
- o   Pledge to deliver the best technical solutions to the industry.
- ·   Specify your core strengths at the top of the resume by which the interviewer can decide whether you are eligible for the position.

For example:

- ·   Looked after the day to day reporting of metrics from project management perspective.
- ·   Played a major role in CMMI implementation.
- ·   Worked extensively with external vendors.
- ·   Well versed with industry standard project management procedures.
- ·   Looking forward to work as a Senior Manager.

This is also a good position to specify your objective or position which makes it clear to the interviewer whether he should call you for an interview. For example, if you are looking for senior positions, specify it explicitly. Any kind of certification, such as, PMI, etc, should be made visible in this section.

- ·   Once you have briefly specified your goals and what you have done, it's time to specify what type of project management activities you have worked with. For example metrics reporting, estimation, preparing project plan etc.
- ·   After that, you can run the interviewer through of your experience (what companies you have worked for, from what date to what date, etc.) This will give an overview of your experience to the interviewer. Now its time to mention all the projects you have worked on till now. This list should be in reverse chronological order, starting with your latest project.

For every project, try to put these things:-

- ·   Project Name/Client name (It's sometimes unethical to mention client names; I leave it on the reader to decide.)
- ·   Team strength for each project.
- ·   Time taken for each project.
- ·   Tools, language, and technology used to complete each project.
- ·   Brief summary of the project. Senior people who have vast experience will tend to lengthen their CV by putting in summaries for all projects. Best for all is to just put in descriptions of the first three projects in reverse chronological order, and the rest can be put forth verbally during the interview. I have seen 15-page CVs, but I honestly doubt whether anyone reads them.
- ·   Finally comes your education and personal details.
- ·   If you are trying for onsite postings, do not forget to mention your passport number.
- ·   There are few who try to make their CVs as long as possible. I personally think that a CV should not be more than 4 to 5 pages long.
- ·   Do not mention your present salary in CV. You can talk about it during the HR-round of your interview.

- When you are writing summaries of projects that you have handled, make it effective by using verbs, such as, managed a team of 5 members, architected the project from start to finish, etc.
- Take 4 to 5 photocopies copies of your resume whenever you go for an interview. You may need them.
- Just in case, take at least 2 passport-size photos with you. You may need them too.
- Carry all your current office documents, especially your salary-slips and joining letter.

Salary Negotiation Skills

Ok, the long and the short of it is that we all do it for money! Not everyone maybe, but still, money matters. And salary negotiations are probably the weakest area of the IT professional. They DO NOT make good negotiators. I have seen so many who at the first instance will smile and say "Negotiable."

So, keep the following key points in mind when negotiating for money:

- Do a study of what the salary trend is. Have some kind of baseline in mind. What is the salary trend based on the number of years of experience? Discuss things with your friends beforehand.
- Do not mention your expected salary on the resume.
- Let the employer first make an offer. Try to delay the salary discussion till the very end.
- If they ask you how much you expect, come out with a figure that is a little towards the higher end and say that it is negotiable. Remember, never say negotiable on the figure that you actually want, the HR guys will always bring it down. So negotiate on what you want +a little bit extra.
- The normal trend is that they look at your current salary and add a little it so that they can pull you in. Do your homework. Say clearly that my present salary is this much and I expect this much. I will not come down below this.
- Do not talk harshly during salary negotiations.
- It's good to aim high. For instance I want a billion dollars every month, but at the same time, be realistic also.
- Some companies have those little hidden costs attached to the salary. Clarify it, rather than be surprised when you get your first pay packet.
- Many companies add extra performance compensations to your basic, which can be surprising at times. So, ask for a detail breakdown beforehand. It is best to discuss in-hand salary, rather than NET or CTC.
- Find out what the frequency of hikes and appraisals is.
- Take everything in writing, go back to your house and have a look with a cool head. Is the offer worth it? Give it a good thought.
- Do not forget that once you have job in hand, you can always go back to your current employer and negotiate.
- Remember, cribbing about the fact that your colleague is getting paid more than you is highly unprofessional. So be careful during interview, or be sportive, or be a good negotiator in the next interview.

- One very important thing is that the best negotiating ground is not the new company that you plan to join, but the old company which you are leaving. So, once you have an offer in hand, go back to your old employees, show them the offer, and only then make your next move. It is my personal experience that negotiating with an old employer is easier than with a new one. Frankly, if approached properly, rarely will anyone will say 'no,' as you have spent quiet some time with them. Just do not be aggressive or egoistic that you have an offer in hand.
- Last but not the least, sometime something's are worth more than money: **JOB SATISFACTION** being one of them. So, if the difference is money is not that much, go for job satisfaction. It is, at times, worth more than money.

Broad Salary Structure

Given below, in a tabular form, is the salary structure in the project management trade. This data is from the perspective of the Indian market. Amounts give below are annual CTCs (Cost-to-Company) of project manager according to grade. Below are the salary ranges for different project management level flavors. We have categorized the same according to small, mid and large scale companies. We have also listed different management level flavors with respect to both these types of companies.

> **Note:** - *The below salary structure is not an industry standard. We have seen some managers getting mind blowing salaries even in small scale companies. The below sheet is from the authors knowledge point of view which he has gained from his friends and IT people he knows in the industry. You can take it as bench mark but not as an IT standard.*

	Mid/Small level IT Companies (CTC p.a.)	Large Scale IT companies (CTC p.a.)
Project Manager	700000 - 800000 INR	800000 - 1200000 INR
Program Manager	We have not seen program manager positions in midscale	1000000 - 1300000 INR
Manager (Mid level)	800000 - 1200000 INR	1300000 - 1500000 INR
Senior Manager	1300000 - 1500000 INR	1400000 - 1800000 INR

Figure: Salary Card for Project manager

Interview Rating Sheet

In the CD, we have provided an Interview Rating MS-Excel sheet. This sheet will help you in gaining an insight into how much you are ready for Software testing, JAVA, .NET , SQL Server , Networking or project management interviews. In the excel sheet, we have thirteen sections:

- Guidelines
- JAVA
- Java Results

- .NET
- .NET Results
- SQL Server
- SQL Server Results
- Software Testing
- Software Testing Results
- Networking
- Networking Results
- Project Management
- Project Management results

The guidelines-sheet defines the guidelines for rating. For every question asked, you can rate yourself on a scale of 1 to 5. The following guidelines are to be followed when you rate yourself:

- 0-You have no idea about the question.
- 1-You know only the definition.
- 2-You know the concept but do not have in-depth knowledge of the subject.
- 3-You know the concept and have partial knowledge of the concept.
- 4-You know the concept and have in-depth knowledge of the subject.
- 5- You are an expert and no one can touch you in this area.

The remaining 10 sections are questions and results. For example, we have the project management section and the project management results Section. The project management section will take in the rating inputs for every question, and project management result will show the output. Same holds true for .NET, JAVA, SQL Server , Software Testing and Networking.

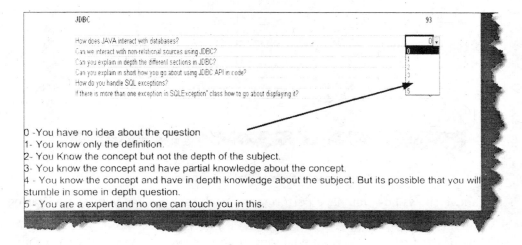

Figure: Rate Yourself

For every question asked, you need to rate yourself. So go through every question and see how good you are. You do not have anyone to supervise you, but remember that at the end of the day it is you who has to clear the interview. So be fair to yourself.

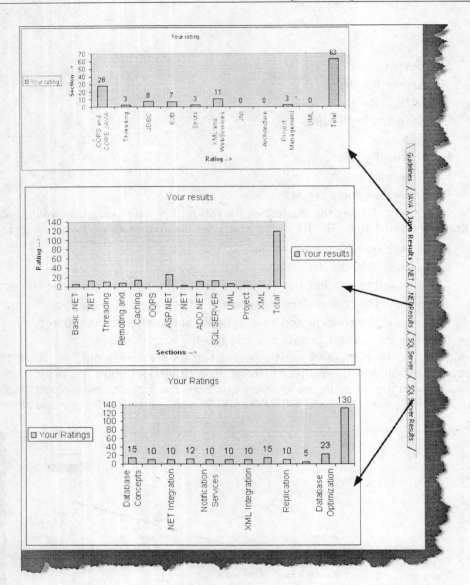

Figure: Overall Rating Values

The figure above shows how you have performed in each section, and your overall rating.

Points to be Remembered During Interviews

- One of the first questions asked during an interview is, "Can you say something about yourself?"
- Can you describe yourself and what you have achieved till now?
- Why do you want to leave your current company?
- Where do you see yourself after 3 years?

- What are your positive and negative traits?
- How do you rate yourself in organization process level implementation on a scale of 1 to 10?
- Are you looking for onsite opportunities? (Be careful do not show your desperation for journeys abroad.)
- Why have you changed so many jobs? (Prepare a decent answer. Do not blame companies and individuals for your frequent changes.)
- Never talk for more than 1 minute straight during an interview.
- Have you worked with industry standard procedures like CMMI , SIX sigma or Agile?
- Do not mention client names in your resume. If asked, say that it's confidential. This brings forth qualities, such as, honesty.
- When you make your resume keep your recent projects at the top.
- Find out what the employer is looking for (router implementation or simple Network troubleshooting) by asking him questions at the start of interview.
- Can you brief us about your family background?
- Do you think that you, being a fresher, can really do this job?
- Have you heard about our company? Say five points about our company? Make sure that you read up on the company you are applying in.
- Can you describe your best project?
- Can you work weekends?
- What is the biggest team size you have worked with?
- Describe your current project.
- How much time will you need to join our organization? What's the notice period in your current organization?
- What certifications do you hold? PMI certification etc,
- Do you have your passport-size photos, final-year marksheet, employment letters from previous companies, last month's salary-slip, passport, and other necessary documents.
- What motivates you the most?
- Why you want to leave your current organization?
- Which type of job gives you the greatest satisfaction?
- What type of environment are you looking for?
- Do you have any experience working in PMO?
- Do you like to work as a team? or as an individual?
- Describe the best manager you have worked for?
- Why should I hire you?
- Have you ever been fired?
- Can you tell us about a few important points that you have learnt from your past project experiences?
- Have you gone through some unsuccessful projects,? If yes, can you tell us why they failed?
- Are you comfortable relocating? If you have personal problems, say 'no' right at the

- beginning, or else within two months you may have to read this book again.
- Do you work late nights? The best answer to this is that you can if there is a project deadline. Do not show that it's your culture to work nights.
- Tell us about your special achievements. Here, say something about your best project.
- Do you have any plans of opening your own software company? Beware! do not start pouring out your Bill Gates' dreams, this can create a wrong impression.

How to Read This Book

If you can read English, you can read this book! Just kidding! There are some legends that will make your reading more effective. Every question has a simple tag that rates the question.

These rating are given by the author, and can vary according to companies and individuals.

(B) Basic Question: 'Basic Question' means that it is a fundamental question and should be answered. For example, 'Explain SDLC cycle?' Stumbling on these questions will rarely see you pass Project Management interviews.

(I) Intermediate Questions: - These are mid-level questions, and you are expected to answer them if you are looking for a decent position in the company.

(A) Advanced Questions: - These are advanced level question that are expected when they are looking for specialists in the field.

> **Note:** *While reading, you will come across sections marked 'Note,' which highlight special points of that section. One advice, do not read this book from start to finish. Go through the index and see which sections you are targeting and revise those.*

Contents

Basics of Project Management

1

Basics of Project Management

(B) Define project?

A project is a temporary endeavor undertaken to create a product or service. Product can be a document, application or a report which can be quantified. Service can be support or Production.

> **Note:** *For readers whose second language is English, let me give the meaning of Endeavor. To exert physical or intellectual strength for the attainment of; to use efforts to effect; to strive to achieve or reach; to try; to attempt.*

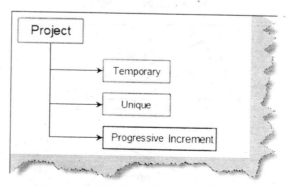

Figure: Characteristics of a project

Let's understand all the three characteristics step by step.

Temporary: Every project is finite. Every project has a beginning and an end. End of the project is reached either when the project fails or it meets the objective.

Unique: Project creates unique deliverables which can be a product, service or results.

Progressive Increments: A progressive increment means developing step by step the project.

(B) Who is a stakeholder?

A stakeholder is anyone who has something to gain or lose as a result of the completion or failure of the project. Stakeholders are people who will benefit from the project. Some of the examples of stake holders are end users, customer who finances the project, project managers and developers. One point to note is it's not necessary that the stake holder is always the end customer it can be the developer and project manager for the project also.

(B) Can you explain Scope triangle?

'Scope triangle' is also termed as 'Quality triangle'. Triangle shows the relationships between three important aspects of the project first is the time to deliver the project, cost which represents the money for the project and what quality/standard you need to maintain in the project. Figure 'Scope triangle' explains how these three aspects form a triangle.

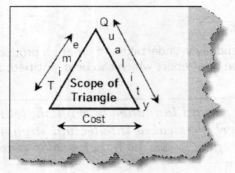

Figure: Scope Triangle

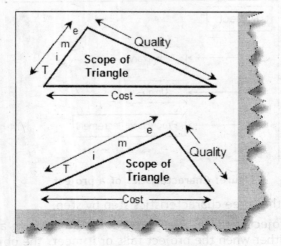

Figure: One factor fixed-normal

In normal situation one of the factors is fixed and the other two can vary. For instance figure 'One factor fixed-normal' shows with one fixed factor and the other varying the triangle still persists. In short if the triangle is complete it means project is under control.

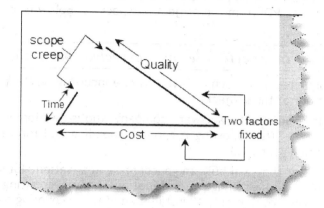

Figure: Two Factor Fixed-Abnormal

Now see figure 'Two factor fixed -abnormal' where the time is less than the other two aspects i.e. cost and quality. You can see how the triangle does not complete by itself. We can term the gap between 'time' and 'quality' as scope creep.

(B) Can you explain what are vision and goals?

Vision is that one statement which abstracts the final aim of the project. Vision is something all the stakeholders in the project agree upon and are always aware while executing the project. Goals form the subset of vision. They represent broader level activities which should be achieved to meet the vision. We can say they are details of a vision. So vision is broad level thinking while goals are low level subset of the vision.

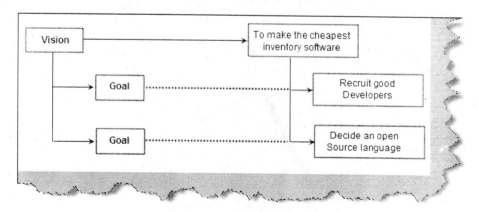

Figure: Vision and Goal

(B) What is ROI?

ROI is a measurement by which we can evaluate the financial value organization will gain from the project. ROI can also be used to measure returns from IT department to a company. In this book we will see ROI from the project perspective. Below is a generic formula for ROI:

$$ROI = (Expected\ profit\ in\ monetary\ terms\ /\ expected\ cost\ of\ the\ project) * 100$$

In one line ROI compares how much cost you will be incurring on the project to the total profit you will get out of the project.

Let's take a simple example of a software company who is developing a simple software accounting application. The following is a rough spending and forecast revenue on the accounting application year wise.

Year 2007: In this year they will built the accounting application. Total rough estimate is 20,000 Dollars. They will be selling per installation of the accounting software for 1500 dollars. Company estimates that only 10 installation of the accounting software will happen in the first year.

Year 2008: In the next year i.e. 2008 we need to only spend 1000$ on the traveling charges of the installation engineer. In this year they expect 13 to 15 installations. So forecasting from minimum sales we assume that only 13 installations will happen, i.e. a net profit of approximately 20,000 dollars.

Year 2009: From year 2009 onwards company expects to have fixed installation of 5 to 6 because of competitors coming in. So the net profit is around 10,000 dollars.

Below figure 'ROI' shows how the ROI calculation with respect to the yearly view. In the below figure you can see we have the statistics and a graph drawn from the statistics. The ROI increases till 20 in 2008 and then again comes down to 10 in 2009.

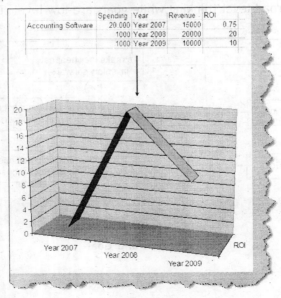

	Spending	Year	Revenue	ROI
Accounting Software	20,000	Year 2007	15000	0.75
	1000	Year 2008	20000	20
	1000	Year 2009	10000	10

Figure: ROI

(B) Can you explain project life cycle?

> **Twist:** *How many phases are there in software project ?*

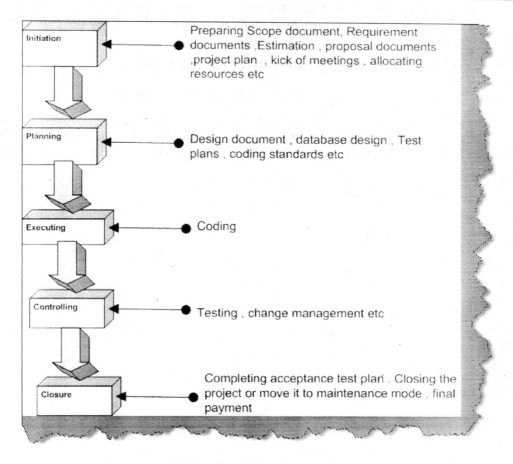

Figure: Life cycle of a project

There are five stages of any project initiating, planning, executing, controlling, and closeout. These are general phases and change according to domain. Example when writing a book we will have the following mappings initiating (contacting publishers, getting copy right etc), planning (Table of contents of book, Number of chapters, tool to use, chapter wise deadlines etc), executing (Actually writing the book), controlling (proof reading, language checks, page alignments etc), and closeout (Finally printing and on the shelf for sale). Therefore, this classification is at very broader level, for software development the above figure shows the mapping.

During Software project management interview, expected answer is requirement phase, design phase, coding phase, testing phase, and project closure. But you can just impress the answer by giving a general answer and then showing the mapping.

(B) People in your team do not meet deadlines or do not perform what are the actions you will take?

In such kind of question, they want to see your delegation skills. The best answer to this question is 'a job of a project manager is managing projects and not problems of people, so I will delegate this work to HR or upper authority'.... Thanks to my Project Manager for this beautiful answer.

(B) Are risk constant through out the project?

> **Note:**   *Never say that risk is high through out the project.*

Risk is high at the start of projects, but by proper POC (Proof of concept), risk is brought in control. Good project managers always have proper risk mitigation plan at the start of project. As the project continues one by one, risks gets eliminated thus bringing down the risk.

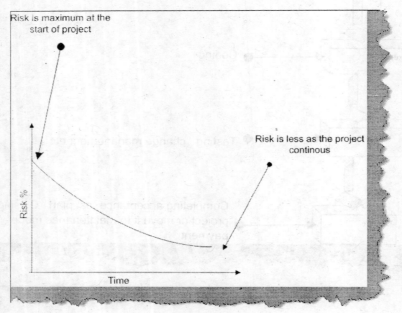

Figure: Risk % according to project phases

(I)   Explain SDLC (Software development Life Cycle) in detail?
(I)   Can you explain waterfall model?
(I)   Can you explain big-bang waterfall model?
(I)   Can you explain phased waterfall model?
(I)   Explain Iterative, Incremental, Spiral, Evolutionary and V-Model?
(I)   Explain Unit testing, Integration tests, System testing and Acceptance testing?

Every activity has a life cycle and software development process is not an exception for the same. Even if you are not aware of SDLC you still must be following it unknowingly. But if a software professional is aware about SDLC he can execute the project in a much controlled fashion. One of the big benefits of this awareness is that hot blooded developers will not start directly execution (coding) which can really lead to project running in an uncontrolled fashion. Second it helps customer and software professional to avoid confusion by anticipating the problems and issues before hand. In short SDLC defines the various stages in a software life cycle.

But before we try to understand what SDLC is all about. We need to get a broader view of the start and end of SDLC. Any project started if it does not have a start and end then its already in trouble. It's like if you go out for a drive you should know where to start and where to end or else you are moving around endlessly.

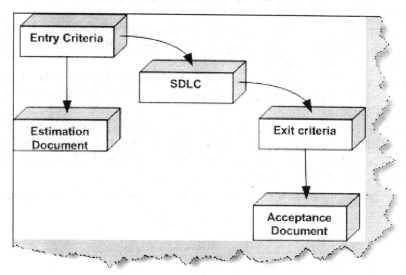

Figure: Entry, SDLC and Exit in action

Above is a more global view of the how the start and end of SDLC. Any project should have entry criteria and exit criteria. For instance a proper estimation document can be an entry criteria condition. That means if you do not have a proper estimation document in place the project will not start. It can be more practical, if half payment is not received the project will not start. So there can be list of points which needs to be completed before a project starts. Finally there should be end of the project also which defines saying that this is when the project will end. For instance if all the test scenarios given by the end customer is completed that means the project is finished. In the above figure we have the entry criteria as an estimation document and exit criteria as a signed document by the end client saying the software is delivered.

Below is the figure that shows typical flow in SDLC which has five main models .As per use project managers can select model for their project.

· Waterfall - Big Bang and Phased model.

· Iterative - Spiral and Incremental model.

Waterfall

Let's have a look on Waterfall model which is basically divided into two subtypes:

· Big Bang waterfall model.

· Phased waterfall model.

As the name suggests Waterfall means flow of water always goes in one direction so when we say waterfall model we expect every phase/stage is freezed.

Big Bang waterfall model

The figure shows waterfall Big Bang model which has several stages and are described as below:

· Requirement stage: This stage takes basic business needs required for the project which is from a user perspective so this stage produces typical word documents with simple points or may be in a form of complicated use case documents.

· Design stage: Use case document / requirement document is the input for this stage. Here we decide how to design the project technically and produce technical document which has Class diagram, pseudo code etc.

· Build stage: This stage follow the technical documents as an input so code can be generated as an output by this stage. This is where the actual execution of the project takes place.

· Test stage: Here testing is done on the source code produced by the build stage and final software is given a green flag. Deliver stage: After succeeding in Test stage the final product/project is finally installed at client end for actual production. This stage is start for the maintenance stage.

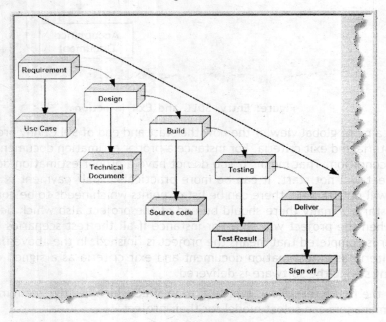

Figure: SDLC in action (Waterfall big bang model)

In water fall big bang model, it is assumed that all stages are freezed that means it's a perfect world. But in actual projects such processes are impractical.

Phased Waterfall model

In this model the project is divided into small chunks and delivered at intervals by different teams. In short, chunks are developed in parallel by different teams and get integrated in the final project. But the disadvantage of this model if there is improper planning may lead to fall of the project during integration or any mismatch of co-ordination between the team may cause huge failure.

Iterative model

Iterative model was introduced because of problems faced in Waterfall model.

Now let's try to have a look on Iterative model which also has a two subtype as follows:

Incremental model

In this model work is divided into chunks like phase waterfall model but the difference is that in Incremental model one team can work on one or many chunks which was unlike in phase waterfall model.

Spiral model

This model uses series of prototype which refine on understanding of what we are actually going to deliver. Plans are changed if required as per refining of the prototype. So every time in this model refining of prototype is done and again the whole process cycle is repeated.

Evolutionary model

In Incremental and Spiral model the main problem is for any changes in between SDLC cycle we need to iterate the whole new cycle. For instance, During the final(Deliver)stage customer demands for change we iterate the whole cycle again that means we need to update all the previous (Requirement, Technical documents, Source code & Test plan) stages.

In Evolutionary model, we divide software into small units which can be earlier delivered to the customer's end which means we try to fulfill the customer's needs. In the later stages we evolve the software with new customers needs.

V-model

This type of model was developed by testers to emphasis the importance of early testing. In this model testers are involved from requirement stage itself. So below is the diagram (V model cycle diagram) which shows how for every stage some testing activity is done to ensure that the project is moving as planned.

For instance,

- In requirement stage we have acceptance test documents created by the testers. Acceptance test document outlines that if these test pass then customer will accept the software.
- In specification stage testers create the system test document. In the coming section system testing is explained in more elaborate fashion.
- In design stage we have integration documents created by the testers. Integration test documents define testing steps of how the components should work when integrated. For instance you develop a customer class and product class. You have tested the

customer class and the product class individually. But in practical scenario the customer class will interact with the product class. So you also need to test is the customer class interacting with product class properly.

In implement stage we have unit documents created by the programmers or testers.

Lets try to understand every of this testing phase in more detail.

Unit Testing

Starting from the bottom the first test level is "Unit Testing". It involves checking that each feature specified in the "Component Design" has been implemented in the component.

In theory an independent tester should do this, but in practice the developer usually does it, as they are the only people who understand how a component works. The problem with a component is that it performs only a small part of the functionality of a system, and it relies on co-operating with other parts of the system, which may not have been built yet. To overcome this, the developer either builds, or uses special software to trick the component into believe it is working in a fully functional system.

Integration Testing

As the components are constructed and tested they are then linked together to check if they work with each other. It is a fact that two components that have passed all their tests, when connected to each other produce one new component full of faults. These tests can be done by specialists, or by the developers.

Integration Testing is not focused on what the components are doing but on how they communicate with each other, as specified in the "System Design". The "System Design" defines relationships between components.

The tests are organized to check all the interfaces, until all the components have been built and interfaced to each other producing the whole system.

System Testing

Once the entire system has been built then it has to be tested against the "System Specification" to check if it delivers the features required. It is still developer focused, although specialist developers known as systems testers are normally employed to do it.

In essence System Testing is not about checking the individual parts of the design, but about checking the system as a whole. In fact it is one giant component.

System testing can involve a number of specialist types of test to see if all the functional and non-functional requirements have been met. In addition to functional requirements these may include the following types of testing for the non-functional requirements:

· Performance - Are the performance criteria met?

· Volume - Can large volumes of information be handled?

· Stress - Can peak volumes of information be handled?

· Documentation - Is the documentation usable for the system?

· Robustness - Does the system remain stable under adverse circumstances?

(I)   What's the difference between system and acceptance testing?

Acceptance Testing

Acceptance Testing checks the system against the "Requirements". It is similar to systems testing in that the whole system is checked but the important difference is the change in focus:

Systems testing checks that the system that was specified has been delivered. Acceptance Testing checks that the system will deliver what was requested.

The customer should always do acceptance testing and not the developer. The customer knows what is required from the system to achieve value in the business and is the only person qualified to make that judgment. This testing is more of getting the answer for whether is the software delivered as defined by the customer. It's like getting a green flag from the customer that the software is up to the expectation and ready to be used.

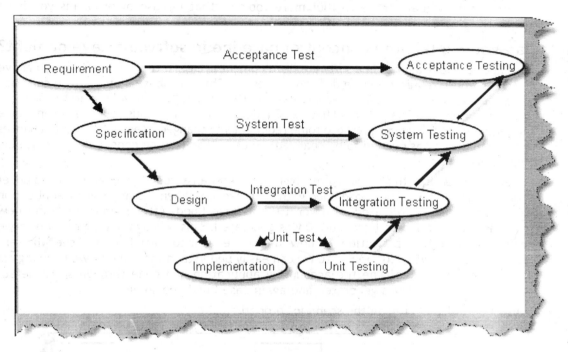

Figure: V model cycle flow

(I)   Which is the best model?

In the previous section we looked through all the models. But in real projects, hardly one complete model can fulfill the entire project requirement. In real projects, tailor model are proven to be the best because they share features from all models such as Waterfall, Iterative, Evolutionary models etc and can fit in to real life time projects. Tailor model are most productive and benefited for many organization. If it's a pure testing project then V model is the best.

(B)   What is CAR (Causal Analysis and Resolution)?

The basic purpose of CAR is to analyze all defects, problems, and good practices/positive triggers in projects, perform a root cause analysis of the same, identify respective corrective and preventive actions, and track these to closure. The advantage of CAR is that root causes are scientifically identified and their corrective and preventive actions are carried out. CAR needs to be performed at project initiation, all phase and project ends and on a monthly basis. Fishbone diagram (You can read about the same in detail in the coming section) is one of the ways you can do CAR.

(B)   What is DAR (Decision Analysis and Resolution)?

Decision Analysis and Resolution is to analyze possible decisions using a formal evaluation process that identifies alternatives against established criteria.

Example in a project you are said to use third party tools so you will not depend on only one tool but evaluate three to four more tools so that in case of problems you have alternatives.

(B)   Can you explain the concept of baseline in software development?

Base lines are logical ends in a software development cycle. For instance let's say you have software whose releases will be done in phases i.e. Phase 1, Phase 2 etc. So you can base line your software product after every phase. In this way you will now be able to track the difference between Phase 1 and Phase 2. Changes can be in various sections for instance the requirement document (because some requirements changed), technical (due to changes the architecture was needed to be changed), Source code (source code change), test plan change and so on.

For example consider the below figure which shows how an accounting application had under gone changes and was then base lined with each version. When the accounting application was released it was released with Ver 1.0 and base lined. After some time some new features where added and version 2.0 was generated. This was again a logical end so we again base lined the application. So now in case we want to track back and see what are the changes from VER 2.0 to VER 1.0 we can easily understand the same as we have logical base lines. After some time the accounting application had gone through some defect removal i.e. VER 3.0 was generated and again base lined and so on.

Below figure depicts the all the scenarios properly.

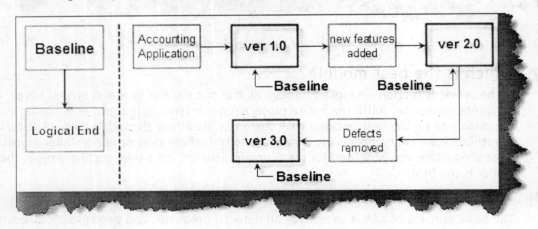

Figure: Base line

Base line is very important from project management perspective it gives a clear cut history of what changes are done to the project. In case of issues we can track back and analyze accordingly.

(B) What is the software you have used for project management?

There are many project management software available in the market but this can vary from company to company Worst it can very from project to project. But Microsoft project is the most used software at this moment. So just brush your skills on Microsoft project, as it's used heavily across industry.

(B) What does a project plan consist?

Project plan is a formal road map document which decides how project executes and how is the project controlled. A project plan should answer the following questions as shown in figure 'Project Plan'.

Why: Why does the project exists first at place?. What is the problem of the customer, why is he funding the project?.

What: What are the major product/deliverables from the project. For instance source, test plans, design documents etc.

Who: Who will be involved in the project and what task will they be working on.

When: When will the project start and when will it finish.

> ***Note:***   *The above points are on a very generic level. For instance why can be a short description of the project, what will be your WBS (read more about WBS in the coming sections) plan, who will be a allocation of resources to the task and when will be a simple GANTT chart or any chart which depicts the schedule of the project. The whole point is that the above points should be covered in a project plan.*

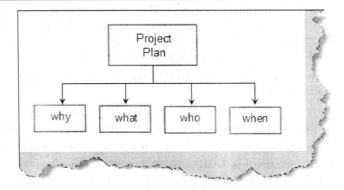

Figure: Project Plan

(B) When do you say the project has finished?

If it's a maintenance project then there is no word finish as such. But we can a project is done when the project manager receives a acceptance sign off of the project.

(B) Can you explain what a PMO office is?

PMO office is an enterprise level department or group for executing standard business processes for project management within the organization. PMO will be responsible to apply project management principles on accepted industry methodologies. Many organizations also see PMO at enterprise level to deal with business initiatives like mergers, acquisitions, and organizational project management policies.

(B) How many members in your team you have handled?

Left to the reader.

(A) Is GANTT chart a project plan?

No, it's a project schedule.

> **Note:** *You can read about GANTT charts in the coming section.*

(B) What is a change request?

Change request is a request which changes the main project requirement which was initially signed off by the end customer.

(B) How did you manage change request in your project?

> **Note:** *In all IT companies Change request is termed as CR. So do not get stunned by the word CR during project management interviews.*

Below diagram 'CR procedure' shows in general how change request is handled. Let us try to understand the same in a detailed manner:

Step 1: The end user or the customer raises a change request.

Step 2: The CR is analyzed by a group of people who understand the business. If they think its worth considering they give an approval saying please go ahead with a detail impact analysis in terms of changes and cost or else it's either deferred or rejected. Many times end users raise change request which does not add much value addition to the business so it's essential that it should once go through a formal review process.

Step 3: Technical IT team does an impact analysis and also estimates how much time it will take to implement the CR.

Step 4: Again a review process is done from the angle of cost and impact. Some times if the cost is too high it's very much possible that the CR can be rejected or deferred.

Step 5: If approved the technical team does the execution and goes ahead with the testing part. There can be two level of testing one is internally (internal testing) and other is from the end customer testing (Acceptance testing). If the acceptance testing goes fine its time to close the CR.

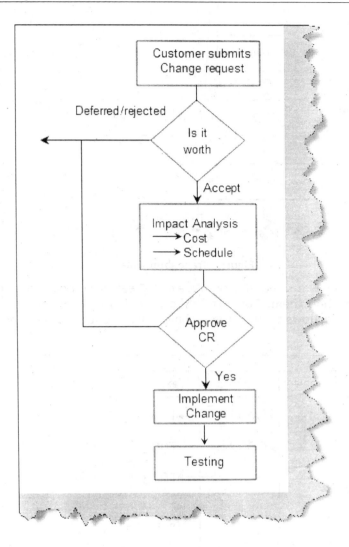

Figure: CR procedure

(B) Can you explain traceability matrix?

Traceability matrix associates requirements with end products which satisfy them. It helps us to authenticate the completeness from the requirement to technical to test plan and finally to the end product. In this way we ensure that none of the requirements are missed out. In short it shows a bird eye view that all requirements have an end product.

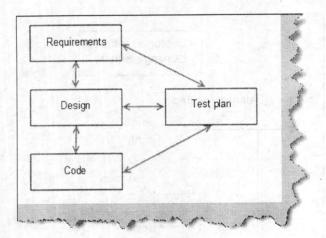

Figure: Traceability Matrix

You can maintain the same in a simple excel sheet or you can have identifiers in every document and link them. For instance below figure shows an abstract view of how requirement r001 flows through the technical documents, test case and then to the final code.

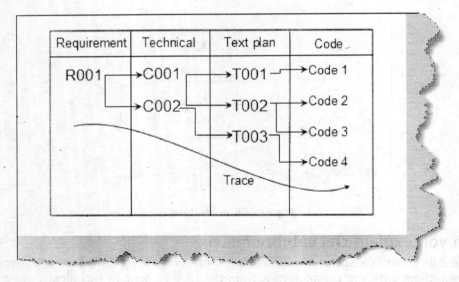

Figure: Overview of Traceability matrix

(I)   What is configuration management?

It's the process of controlling and monitoring change as the software evolves. In one sentence it is tracking of the software changes as the software moves ahead. It's a process of controlling and documenting changes that happen in a software project. Some of the queries which a proper configuration management will answer are as follows:

- · When was the change done?
- · Why was the change done?
- · Who did the change?
- · What was the change done?

For instance below figure 'VSS CM' shows a simple configuration management done using Visual source. Developers where advised that when they check in the source code they should be checking in with all the below details.

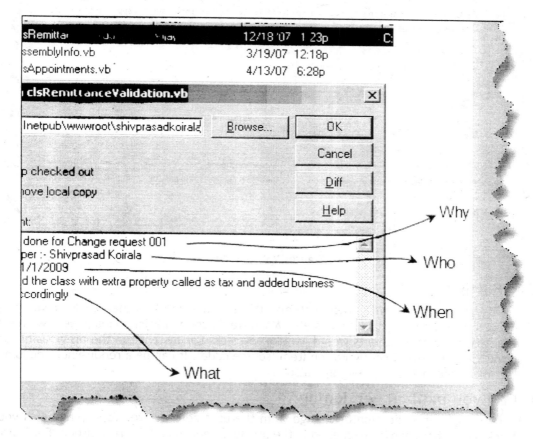

Figure: VSS CM

When you derive the changes done on the project source code as shown in below figure 'VSS changes' you can see the importance of CM. We are able to trace who has done it, what was done etc.

```
$/shivproject/BaseLine/Sourcecode/Solution1/shiv-project/Interface/ClsApplicantAbstract/Interface.vb
***************** Version 7 *****************  ——————→ version 7
User: vijay          Date: 11/18/07  Time:   3:57p
Checked in $/shivproject/BaseLine/Sourcecode/Solution1/shiv-project/Interface/ClsApplicantAbstract
Comment:

***************** Version 6 *****************  ——————→ version 6
User: vijay          Date: 11/15/07  Time:   9:13p
Checked in $/shivproject/BaseLine/Sourcecode/Solution1/shiv-project/Interface/ClsApplicantAbstract
Comment:
  Added new property called "Action"
***************** Version 5 *****************  ——————→ version 5
User: vijay          Date: 11/15/07  Time:   5:09p
Checked in $/shivproject/BaseLine/Sourcecode/Solution1/shiv-project/Interface/ClsApplicantAbstract
Comment:
  Added new Class "clsApplicantDESdetailsAbstract" to collect all the
DES fields

********************
Label: Baseline22OCT2007
User: Ajay           Date: 10/22/07  Time:   7:26p
Labeled 'Baseline22OCT2007'
Label comment:
  Holding Accounts
Reporting webservices
New Ghana webservice
***************** Version 4 *****************  ——————→ version 4
User: vijay          Date: 10/09/07  Time:   8:32p
Checked in $/shivproject/BaseLine/Sourcecode/Solution1/shiv-project/Interface/ClsApplicantAbstract
Comment:
  REMOVED NEW CLASS clsRefundsAbstraction
***************** Version 3 *****************  ——————→ version 3
User: vijay          Date: 10/09/07  Time:   5:32p
Checked in $/shivproject/BaseLine/Sourcecode/Solution1/shiv-project/Interface/ClsApplicantAbstract
Comment:
  added new class clsRefundsAbstract
```

Figure: VSS changes

(I)   What is CI?

CI also termed as configuration items. It's a collection of objects like requirement document, source code, test plans etc. When we do configuration management we need to first identify which objects would we like to track. For instance in the previous question using VSS we tracked configuration item 'source code'. It can be a requirement document, technical document or a test plan also.

(B)   Can you explain versioning?

Versioning is an indication of change from the user perspective. Versioning helps you to track back what changes happened in the previous version and the recent one. For instance below figure 'Accounting Software' shows three releases of accounting software version. Every release has some changes which is logical from the user's perspective. So at any point if we want to know what software feature the current software has, we need to just know which version is installed in his PC.

(I)   Can you explain the concept of sign off?

Sign off is an official agreement for the scope of a project with the end user. For instance if you have a requirement document you would like to the user to given an official approval saying that this is the scope of the project and any deviation from the same will be taken and as change request (read more about change request in the previous questions).

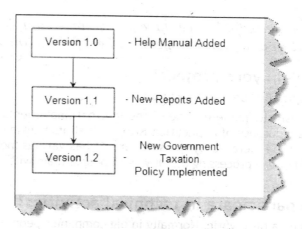

Figure: Accounting Software

(B)   How will you start a project?

This answer depends completely on how you want to answer and to be truthful many interviewers expect different answers. From our perspective an interviewer expects that a project should start with a kick of meeting in which the project manager communicates the project plan to his team members. But again many people expect different answers some expect requirement sign off, some expect project plan etc. This answer is really subjective.

(I)   What is an MOU?

MOU stands for Memorandum of Understanding. It's a legal document which describes agreement between two parties to work on a common line of action. For instance below are some points which can come in to a MOU:

- If a developer is needed by the end client for onsite traveling charges will be paid by vendor.
- Acceptance testing should be performed by the user in 3 weeks after the build is delivered.
- Warranty period of the software after acceptance phase is two weeks.
- If any developer has to be rolled out a one month notice needs to be served.

(B)   What where the deliverables in your project?

This answer depends on your project. Below are deliverables which are mostly expected from every project:

- Requirement document
- Technical document
- Test plans
- Source code

But a complicated project can have extra deliverables like traceability metrics, MOU (Memorandum of Understanding) etc.

> **Note:** *In the documents folder we have given some sample documents from a simple chat application perspective. Feel free to analyze the same.*

(B) Can you explain your project?

Left to the readers. But below is a sample.

This project is basically made for one of the international clients whose main business is banking. The main purpose of application is to unite all its banking agents in to one unified process which will be dictated by the software. It has various modules like voucher data entry screen, end of day processing etc. It was 15 people team with two team leads reporting to me.

(B) Do you also participate in technical activities?

This answer can be a bit cryptic. Normally in big companies people do not expect a project manager to be technically strong. If a project manager is showing too much of technical inclination it can create negative impact during interview. A good answer would be if time demands I had to get down in to technical at least from a bird view angle.

(B) How did you manage code reviews?

This answer is again subjective. Below are some popular ways of doing the same.

Peer review: From the same team peers review each others code.

External review: In this we bring in other external parties in to picture who can do code reviews. For instance you can call some from the other project or probably your organization has its own architecture department who does code reviews.

(I) You have team member who does not meets his deadlines how do you handle it?

This is again a subjective answer. Just do not be harsh like i will remove him from the project etc. From my point of view my answer will be i will give him ample chances with proper training if still he does not come to the mark I will give him a polite roll off from the project.

(I) Did you have project audits if yes how was it handled?

Normally in big organization the SQA department does the audit. They basically have a checklist of documents which needs to be delivered by the project. If any document is left out then they raise a NCR (Non-Conformance report) for the same, which then needs to be closed by the project manager within a stipulated time span.

(I) What is a non-conformance report (NCR)?

Answered in the above question.

(I) How did you estimate your project?

Read the estimation chapter for more details

(B) How did you motivate your team members?

This is again a subjective answer. You can say salary raise, onsite opportunities, role change etc.

(I) Did you create leaders in your team if yes how?

Very tricky question...Think about a nice answer sometimes these types of question becomes job deciding factor for a project manager.

(I) how did you confirm that your modules are resource independent?

These kinds of questions really judge if the project manager has really worked as project manager. In my project we used to have weekly knowledge transfer session which would ensure that every module is know to every developer. Second we used to also rotate modules on regular basis this ensured that we do not have developers tied up to a module.

> **Note:** But again this answer is subjective. Some can say we had proper documentation at place, some can say we had code properly commented etc.

(B) Was your project show cased for CMMI or any other project process standardization?

Left to the reader. In case you say yes you should know how the project fulfilled CMMI activities.

(I) what are the functions of the Quality Assurance Group (QAG)?

In bigger organization it's a different body by itself which assures that a project is performing activities which verify the quality of product. It assures that the project provides evidence that it's adhering to quality.

(B) Can you explain milestone?

Milestone indicates a logical completion for work package or a phase. For instance some of the milestones are version wise milestone, phase wise milestone, module wise milestone etc.

(I) How did you do assessment of team members?

Every organization has assessment structure in place. Most of the organization follows the method of setting KRA (Key result areas) and goals for an individual and then measuring the same at the end of the year. KRA are nothing but objectives which have defined goals with numbers. For instance below figure 'KRA' shows how a manager has defined a typical KRA for him with goal. You can also see how every goal is measurable to avoid any kind of confusion during year end assessment.

KRA	Goal	Acheived	Rating Definition
Project Management	3	2	5 - Outstanding Performance
Team Interaction	4	3	4 - Exceeds expectation occasionally
Proactiveness	4	3	3 - Consistently performs as per expectation
Customer Interaction	4	4	2 - Meets expectation ocasionally
			1 - Need Improvements

Figure: KRA

Note: *All big companies follow KRA way of assessment.*

(B) What does entry and exit criteria mean in a project?

Entry and exit criteria are a must for the success of any project. If you do not know from where to start and where to finish then your goals are not clear. By defining exit and entry criteria you define your boundaries. For instance you can define entry criteria that the customer should give the requirement document or acceptance plan. If these entry criteria's are not met then you will not start the project. On the other end you can also define exit criteria for your project. For instance one of the common exit criteria's in all project is that customer has successfully executed the entire Acceptance Test plan.

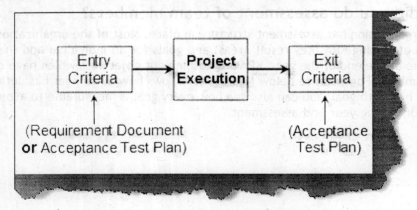

Figure: Entry and exit criteria

(B) How much are you as leader and how much are you as PM?

Again a subjective answer. From my point of view a good PM is 50 percent leader ship and 50 PM. We can give you many examples where the project sustained not due to metrics or process but by good leadership.

(B) How do you handle conflicts between project people having conflicts?

It really depends on what kind of conflict it is. The most difficult conflict is the EGO conflict. My answer will be on this I would put them on modules which are isolated. So that they have least interaction.

(B) In your team you have highly talented people how did you handle their motivation?

This again completely depends on what the individual is looking at. For instance some people would like to have onsite opportunities; some would like to get promotion, salary increase etc. If the individual is really helpful on the project and there is opportunity to meet his motivation I will go ahead with it.

(B) How can you balance between underperforming and outperforming people ?

In all projects what I have done is always paired a underperforming with an outperforming developer. I have also instructed and monitored to ensure that the underperforming person does not act like a parasite on the outperforming developer. Over a period of time you can easily see that underperforming person becoming one of the key memebers of the project.

(I) You need to make choice between delivery and quality what's your take?

From my point of the first choice would be quality. Even if there is a time constraint we should try to implement as much as quality possible within that time frame.

2
Risk Management

(B)   Define risk?

Risk is an event which can lead to a financial loss in the project.

(I)   What is risk break down structure?

It's same like WBS but the main aspect is the risk and not the project. For instance below figure 'RBS' shows how the risk for accounting project is categorized in a hierarchical manner.

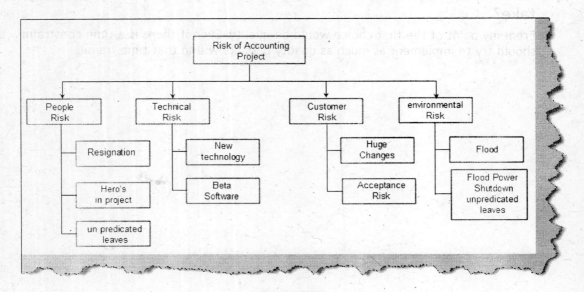

Figure: RBS

RBS can vary from organization to organization and project to project. For instance same accounting project RBS can be viewed in a different manner as shown in figure 'Different View of RBS'.

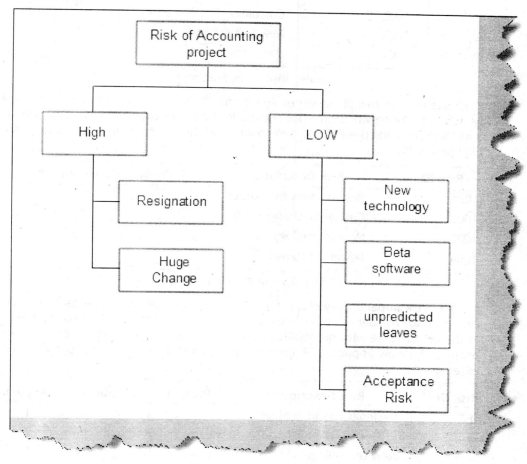

Figure: Different View of RBS

(I)   How did you plan your risk?

Below figure 'Risk management' shows how the risk is identified and planned. It's possible that every organization or we will say rather every project differ in the way they plan risk. We will look in to the way generally a process oriented organization will look at how risk is planned.

Identify risk: In this phase we describe risk with a detail description and assign a risk id number to the same. This is normally done in discussion with team members and stake holders.

Risk ID	Risk Description
1001	Resignations in project
1002	Customer changes a lot.
1003	New technology
1004	Power shutdown

Table: Risk Identification

- **Evaluate risk:** In this phase we evaluate importance of every risk. For this we can put what's the rate by which this risk occurs. In the below table we have assigned 1, 2 and 3 as the rating for the risk. So 1 → low probability, 2 → medium probability and 3 → high probability.

Risk ID	Risk Description	Probability of failure
1001	Resignations in project	3
1002	Customer changes a lot.	2
1003	New technology	1
1004	Power shutdown	2

Table: Give probability rating

- **Analyze risk impact:** Only occurrence does not conclude how important the risk is, we need to also consider the other aspect what can be the impact of the risk on the project. In the below table with probability we have also defined the impact of the risk on the project. 1→ Low impact, 2 → medium impact and 3 → will impact project to a great extent.

Risk ID	Risk Description	Probability of failure	Impact
1001	Resignations in project	3	1
1002	Customer changes a lot.	2	2
1003	New technology	1	1
1004	Power shutdown	2	3

Table: Give impact rating

- **Prioritize risk:** In this phase we logically organize the risk so that we can deal with the same in a prioritized manner. One of the ways we use to define priority is by adding probability and impact. You can find the last column priority is the total of probability + impact.

Risk ID	Risk Description	Probability of failure	Impact	Priority
1001	Resignations in project	3	1	4
1002	Customer changes a lot.	1	2	3
1003	New technology	1	1	2
1004	Power shutdown	2	3	5

Table: Depending on probability and impact decide priority

Depending on the priority we again rearrange the risk. Below table shows the risk now arranged in a prioritized way. This gives us a logical way of dealing with the risks.

Risk ID	Risk Description	Priority
1004	Power shutdown	5
1001	Resignations in project	4
1002	Customer changes a lot.	3
1003	New technology	2

Table: Rearranging risk according to priority

Plan for mitigating risk: Once we have arranged the risk its time to see how we solve the same. In this phase for every risk we list down what is our action or mitigation for the same.

Risk ID	Risk Description	Risk Mitigating plan
1004	Power shutdown	Put backup servers on different geographical locations.
1001	Resignations in project	Should have weekly knowledge transfer plan so that project does not depend on one resource.
1002	Customer changes a lot.	Requirement documents and acceptance plan should be signed off before starting the project.
1003	New technology	Before starting the project every one in the team should go through a proper training on the new technology.

Table: Mitigation plan for risk

Monitor and control risk: This is an on going phase where every risk is tracked and new risk if they come in they are added and prioritized by doing impact analysis.

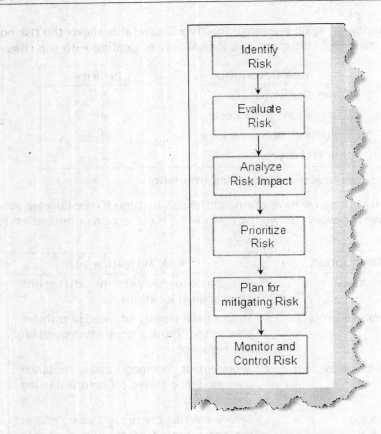

Figure: Risk Management

> **Note:**   *One of the important points which an interviewer will like to see is how the risk was prioritized. In the above explanation we have done the same by adding probability and impact, but it can vary. For instance in many of the organization it can be done by having joint meeting with stake holders where the risk will be prioritized.*

(I)   What is DR, BCP and contingency planning?

DR (disaster recovery) or DRP (Disaster recovery plan) is also referred as BCP (business process contingency plan).BCP describes how an organization should deal with potential disaster. This disaster can be an event which stops the continuation of normal operation. Every business can face incidents which can stop the normal operation from continuing. BCP and DR can also be termed as contingency plan.

3

Schedule Management

(B) Can you explain WBS?

WBS (Work Breakdown Structure) is a structured way of breaking / decomposing project in to various components. In one sentence WBS is a way to breakdown project in to logical lower level details. Below figure 'WBS' shows how a typical WBS looks like. There are six levels till where we can drill down and breakdown the job structure.

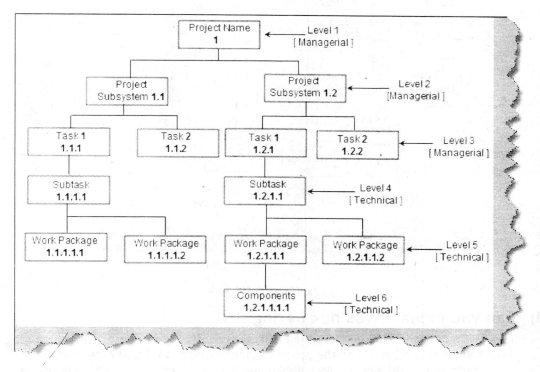

Figure: WBS

Level 1: The first level is the project name or the name of the assignment.

Level 2: Level 2 represents the subsystem which will make up the project.

Level 3: Level 3 shows the task to be performed to complete the subsystem from a managerial aspect.

Level 4: The main task is further broken down in to sub tasks from a technical aspect.

Level 5: This is the final deliverable also termed as work package.

Level 6: These are components needed to form the work package.

From Level 1 to Level 3 are all managerial activities. From Level 4 to Level 6 are all technical activities.

Below figure 'WBS for CPU' shows detail breakdown for assembling a CPU of a computer.

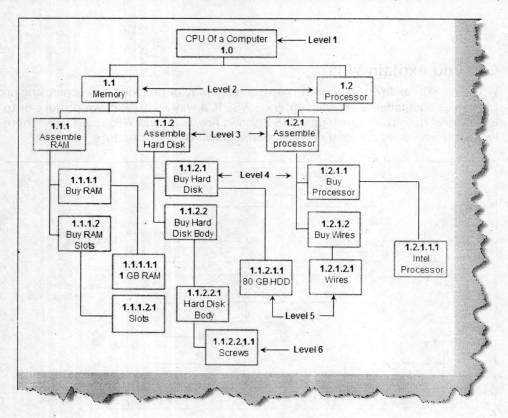

Figure: WBS for CPU

(B) Can you explain WBS numbering?

The first number in WBS denotes the project. For instance in figure 'WBS numbering' we have show the number '1' as the project number which is further extended according to level. Numbering and numeric and alphanumeric or combination of both. Figure 'Different Project Number' shows the project number is '528'.

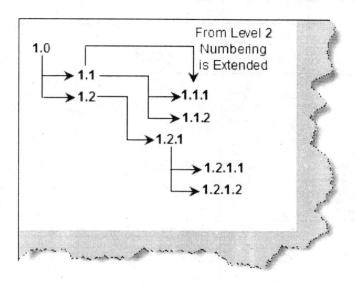

Figure: WBS Numbering

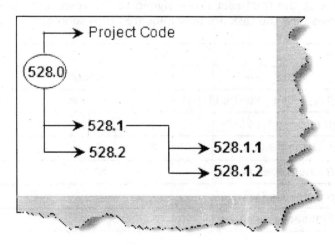

Figure: Different Project Number

(B) How did you do resource allocation?

This answer can vary from individual to individual. But here's how we think it should work. There are two steps for doing resource allocation:

·   Break up the project in to WBS and extract the task from the same. For instance below figure 'Task from WBS' shows how we have broken the accounting project in to small section and the final root is the tasks.

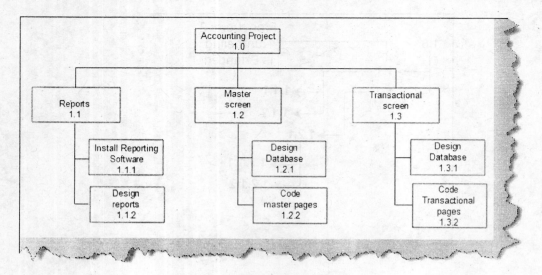

Figure: Task from WBS

Now the tasks at the final root are assigned to the resources. Table 'Assign task to resource' shows how the task are now allocated to resource.

WBS Task	Resource
Install reporting software (1.1.1)	Ramesh
Design reports (1.1.2)	Jack
Design Database (1.2.1)	Shiv
Code master pages (1.2.2)	Sham
Design Database (1.3.1)	Anil
Code Transactional pages (1.3.2)	Sanjana

Figure: Assign task to resource

(I)   Can you explain the use of WBS?

Below is a pictorial view of numerous uses of WBS.

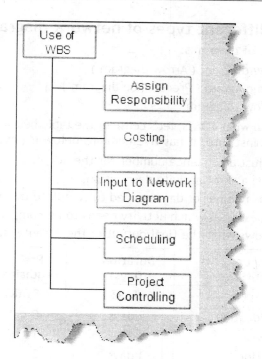

Figure: Use of WBS

One of the main uses of WBS is for scheduling. WBS forms as a input to network diagrams from scheduling aspect.

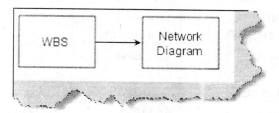

Figure: WBS and Network

(B) Can you explain network diagram?

Network diagram shows logical relationship between project activities. Network diagram helps us in the following ways:

- It helps us understand which activity is independent of other activity. For instance you can start coding/execution of transactional screens with out master screens being completed. This also gives an other view saying that you can execute both the activities in a parallel fashion.

- Network diagram also gives list of activities which can not be delayed. Like we can delay the master screens of a project, but not the transactional.

(B) What are the different types of network diagram?

There are two types of diagrams:

- Activity on Arrow diagram (Arrow diagram)
- Activity on Node diagram (Precedence diagram)

AOA (Activity on Arrow) diagram

Before we understand what AOA is, let's consider the table below which has list of activities to start a computer institute. It has five columns below is description about the same:

- First column is just a sequence number for the activity.
- Second column is a short activity description,
- Third column has number of days needed to complete the activity.
- Fourth column describes which activity needs to be completed to start this activity
- Fifth column shows what the final output of the activity is.

Activity No	Activity Description	Duration (Days)	Pre-requisite	Finished Activity
0	Start project	START	START	START
1	Decide a location	5 days	0	Location Fixed
2	Sign the lease	1 day	1	Agreement Signed
3	Paint Interior	3 days	2	Interior Ready
4	Fix Furniture	20	3	Institute finished
5	Get Faculties	6 days	0	Recruitment done
6	Prepare Course Material	10 days	8	Course designed
7	Buy Computers	2 days	5	Computer bought
8	Install Software	1 day	7	Software Installed
9	Advertise	2 days	3	Ad displayed in news paper
10	Enroll Students	1 day	9	Student enrolled
11	Start Batch	END	END	END

Table: Computer institute Activity list

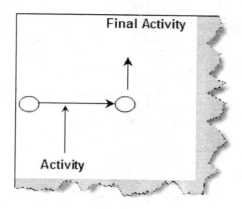

Figure: AOA

As the name suggests Activity on Arrow (i.e. AOA) which means arrows represent activity and the nodes represent finished activities. Figure 'AOA' represents how the activity is shown on the arrow and how the node shows the finished activity. So the node represents completed activities and arrows represent activities.

So let's join the activities and nodes defined in table 'Computer Institute Activity List'. Figure 'AOA for Computer Institute' shows how the AOA diagram is built. We have put the activities on the arrow and the nodes represent the finished activity. On the arrow itself we have put the number of days for every activity.

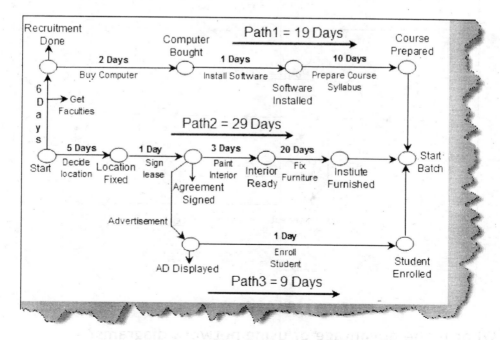

Figure:AOA for Computer Institute

AON (Activity on Node) diagram

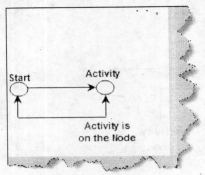

Figure: AON

In AOA we view Activity on arrow while in AON we view Activity on the Node. So the change of thinking shifts from viewing activities as events (AON) rather than activities happening between milestones.

Figure 'AON' represents the same in a pictorial manner. Below is the same redrawn AON diagram for the computer institute activity.

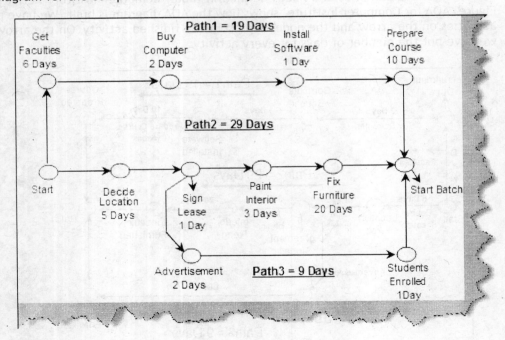

Figure: AON for Computer Institute

(B) What is the advantage of using network diagrams?

Network diagrams help us in the following ways:

- Helps us find our critical / non-critical activities. So if we know our critical activities we would like to allocate our critical people on the critical task and medium performing people on the non-critical activities.

- This also helps us to identify which activities we can run in parallel, thus reducing the total project time.

(B) Can you explain Arrow diagram and Precendence diagram?

AOA (discussed previously) is nothing but Arrow Diagram and AON (as discussed in the previous question) is nothing but precendence diagram.

(B) What are the different types of Network diagrams?

As discussed in the previous section we have two types of network diagrams one is AON (Activity Networks) and other is AOA (Arrow Networks). Below figure 'Types of Network Diagrams' shows the classification in a more visual format. CPM / CPA (Critical Path Method / Critical Path Analysis) and PERT (Program Evaluation and Review Technique) come under Arrow networks. PDM (Precedence Diagrams) comes under activity diagram.

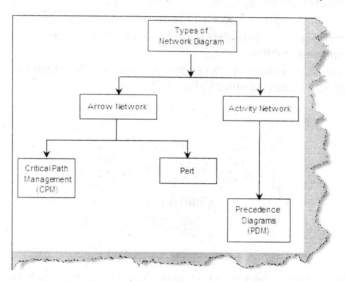

Figure: Types of Network Diagrams

(B) Can you explain Critical path?

CPA / CPM (Critical path analysis / method) are an effective way to analyze complex projects. A project consists of set of activities. CPA represents the critical set of activities to complete a project. Critical path helps us to focus on essential activities which are critical to run the project. Once we identify the critical activities we can devote good resources and prioritize the same accordingly. CPA also gives us a very good basis for scheduling and monitoring for progress. One of the most important thing it does is allows the project manager to concentrate on important activities.

Critical Path is the path which takes the longest time. In the above example we have three paths (please refer AOA for computer institute or AON for computer institute in the previous questions) path1, path2 and path3. Let's sum up the number of days allocated on those paths, so path1 = 19 days, path2 = 29 days and path3 = 9 days. Both figures also show the number of days required on the path.

So path2 is the longest path on the network diagram and also the most important path. In short path2 is the critical path and this method is termed as Critical Path Method /Analysis. Putting in other words the task on the critical path needs careful monitoring and any delays on the critical path will lead to delay of the project. You can easily visualize from the CPM diagram that we if we do not decide location, sign a lease, fix interior and paint we will not have the actual institute at place in given time span.

(l)   Can you define EST, LST, EFT, LFT?

CPM (Critical Path Method) uses the following times for an activity.

- (EST)Early start Time is the earliest time the activity can begin.
- (LST)Late start Time is the latest time the activity can begin and still allow the project to be completed on time.
- (EFT) Early finish Time is the earliest time the activity can end.
- (LFT) Late finish Time is the latest time the activity can end and still allow the project to be completed on time.

We will use the same example of the computer institute described in the previous example for calculating and understanding EST and EFT.

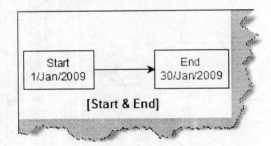

Figure: Start and End

According to CPM calculation the start date should be minimum 1-Jan-2009 and maximum end date is 30-jan-2009. Our EST, EFT, LST and LFT should fall between these lines.

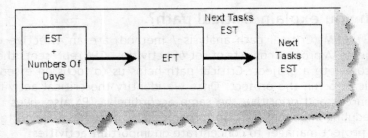

Figure: Forward Calculation

First we need to calculate EST and EFT. EST and EFT are calculated using the forward pass methodology. Figure 'EST and EFT' shows how the forward calculation works. We add "0" to the start date i.e. 1-Jan-2009 which becomes the EST of 'Get Faculties'. 'Get Faculties' task takes the 6 days and adds to EST which gives us 7-Jan-2009 which is the EFT for 'Get Faculties'. EFT becomes the EST of the next task i.e. 'Buy Computers'. Again we add number of days of 'Buy Computers' task to get EFT and so on. In short EFT is calculated by subtracting number of days from EST. EFT of this task becomes the EST of the next task.

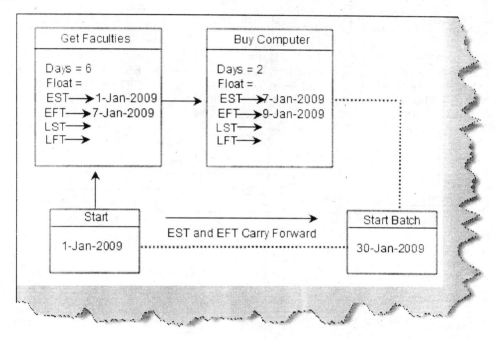

Figure: EST and EFT

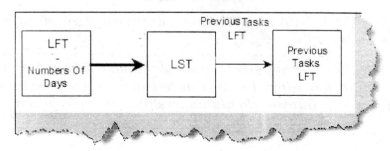

Figure: Backward Calculation

In order to calculate LST and LFT we need to calculate backward from the dead line date.

Figure 'LST and LFT' show how the calculation actually happens. As concluded previously the latest date till which the institute should be ready is 30-Jan-2009. The latest dead line date becomes the LFT of the last activity i.e. 'Prepare Course'. We subtract the number of days from the LFT and get LST of 'Prepare Course' activity which is 20-Jan2009. LST of this activity becomes the LFT of the activity which needs to finish before this i.e. 'Install Software' and so on. Figure 'Backward Calculation' shows how the calculation moves. LST of the current task is LFT minus number of days. Current Activity LST is then assigned to the previous task's LFT.

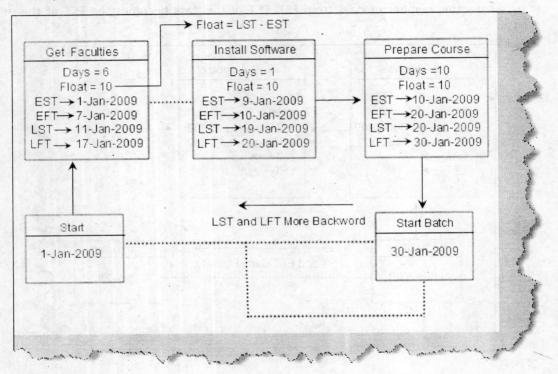

Figure: LST and LFT

Below figure 'EST, EFT, LST and LFT' shows the complete figure after the full calculation forward and backward.

> **Note:** *Try calculating manually to understand how we reached to every figure in the diagram below. In real time scenario you will be using a tool...So do not worry. But you should understand the concept that's important.*

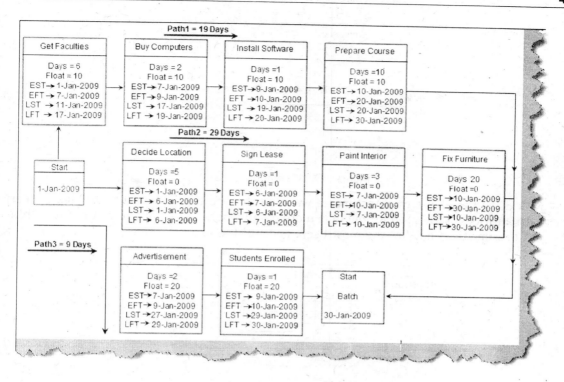

Figure: EST, EFT, LST and LFT

(B) Can you explain Float and Slack?

Float (also known as slack, total float and path float) is computed for each task by subtracting the EFT from the LFT (or the early start from the late start). Float is the amount of time the task can slip without delaying the project finish date. Free float is the amount of time a task can slip without delaying the early start of any task that immediately follows it. In the previous question figure 'EST, EFT, LST and LFT' we have computed the float for every activity. For instance 'Get Faculties' has a slack of 10, 'Advertisement' task has a slack of 20 days and so on.

(B) Can you explain PERT?

PERT is again a network diagram. In CPM the activity durations are based on historic data which has been performed many times. But what if an activity is not performed and this is the first time the activity is performed in the organization, that's when PERT comes to help. CPM is used when the time lines of the activities are determestic while PERT is used when the timelines are not determestic.

PERT uses three time estimates to come to a conclusion regarding time estimates for a activity.

Optimistic Time (a): It's the shortest time in which the activity can be completed.

Pessimistic Time (b): It's the longest time an activity might require.

Most Likely Time (m): It's the completion time which has the highest probability.

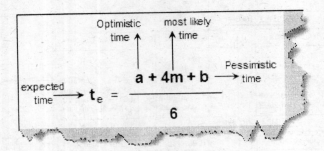

Figure: PERT Computations

Now using the above three estimates we can calculate the expected time. Figure 'Pert Computations' shows the formulae in more detail where 'a' is the optimistic time, 'b' is the pessimistic time, 'm' the most likely and 'te' the expected time.

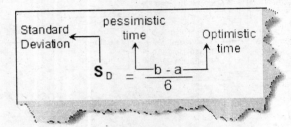

Figure: Standard Deviation

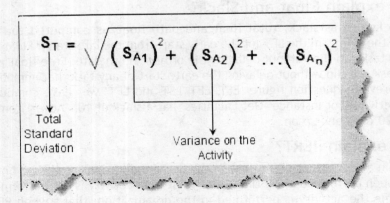

Figure: Total Standard Deviation

Other than expected time there are two more important formula's one is calculating the 'standard deviation (S_d)' and the other is 'total standard deviation (S_t)'. Both the formulas are given in the figure 'Standard Deviation' and 'Total Standard Deviation'. Terminology 'a','b' and 'c' remain same. SA1, SA2 are standard deviations which are calculated on the individual activity.

Let's not talk about theory and let's apply the above fundamentals to our institute project.

What we will do is apply the PERT fundamentals to two different probabilities only on the CPM path of the computer institute. Below figure shows the two probability and the calculations. We can see from the calculations the two probabilities one and two. We can also see the standard deviation of probability one is less than probability two. So probability one has more stability and can hence become our valid plan. Apply the formulas (PERT, T_e, S_d and S_t) explained previously to the diagram.

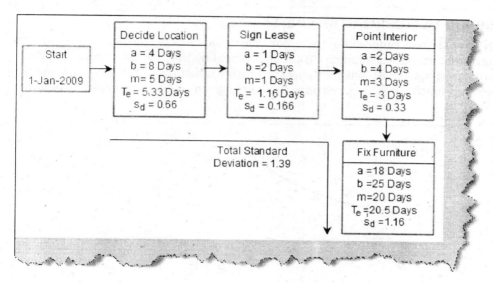

Figure: Probability One

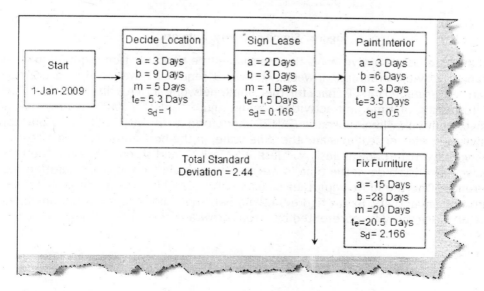

Figure: Probability Two

(B)   Can you explain GANTT chart?

GANTT chart is a time and activity bar chart. Gantt charts are easy-to-read charts that display the project schedule in task sequence and by the task start and finish dates. Gantt charts are simple chart which display the project schedule in task sequence and by the task start and finish dates. Lets consider the below given simple four activity networkv figure.

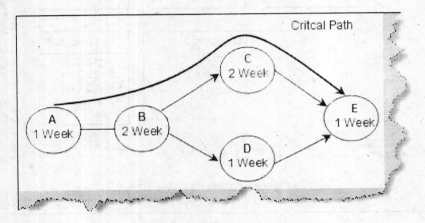

Figure: Simple Activity Network

We have circled the activity and also mentioned the time duration required in weeks. For instance Activity A requires 1 week, Activity B requires 2 weeks and so on. Now let's construct a simple GANTT chart for the simple network activity diagram. GANTT chart is an illustration of time and activities. Below figure 'GANTT CHART' is how the network activity will look when viewed in GANTT chart format. In GANTT chart we put down the activities in the vertical axis and the time scale on the horizontal axis. So on the vertical axis we have listed down 'Task A', 'Task B', 'Task C' and so on. While on the horizontal axis we have listed down the time in weeks. There is one more column duration added for reference. One the most important component in GANTT chart is the activity bar which represents an activity. Below figure 'Activity Bar' shows how we represent an activity. The start of the activity is represented by a top arrow and the end by a down arrow.

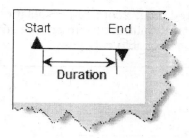

Figure: Activity Bar

So we list down all activities and start drawing the activity bar according to duration.

Once done the final output is as shown in figure 'GANTT chart'. The top bar shows the total activity period. Dependencies are shown by one arrow connecting to the other arrow; we have circled how the dependencies are shown. Task B can only start if task A is completed. GNATT chart is a helpful way to communicate schedule information to top management since it provides an easy-to-read visual picture of the project activities.

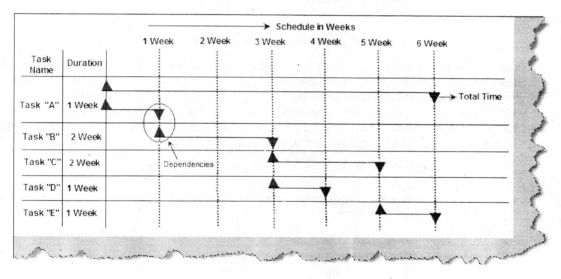

Figure: GANTT Chart

(I) What is the disadvantage of Gantt chart?

It does not show clear dependencies/relationships between tasks, for instance, which task comes first, then second, and so on. It also fails in showing the critical and non-critical tasks. GANTT chart is best used to show summary of the whole project to the top management as it does not show detail information for every activity.

(I) What is Monte-Carlo simulation?

Monte-Carlo helps us to forecast future models depending on range of possible inputs. For instance to complete a project we might have different range of time minimum time, maximum time and estimated time. Monte-carlo simulation runs over these ranges of input values and gives us different possibilities the project can end up to. It can tell you depending on these ranges what are the possible outcomes.

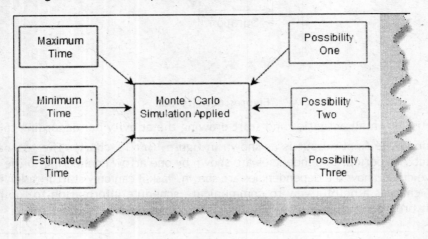

Figure: Monte-Carlo Applied

In Monte-Carlo simulation random value is selected from the range and possibility / model is generated. This model is saved and then the second random value is selected and so on. For instance consider the below figure 'Task1 and Task2'. 'Task2' can be finished only when 'Task1' is completed. We have also chosen the min and max range in which both the task can be completed. 'Task1' can be completed in a minimum time of 1 day and maximum of 3 days. 'Task2' can be completed in minimum 2 days and in maximum 4 days.

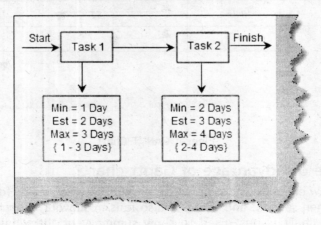

Figure: Task1 and Task2

Now let's apply Monte Carlo simulation. Below figure 'Monet Carlo on Both Tasks' shows the different combinations.

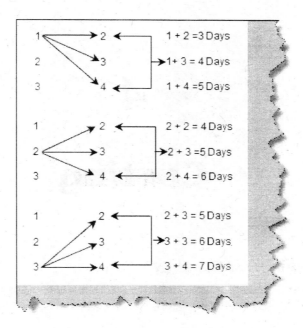

Figure: Monte Carlo on Both Tasks

Now let's collect the number of times the days have occurred. Below figure 'Number of Possibilities' shows that 5 days has occurred the most times. There is a high possibility that task1 and task2 will be completed in 5 days.

Numbers Of Days	Number Of Times
3	1
4	2
5	3
6	2
7	1

← Most Probable

Figure: Number of possibilities

4

Costing

(B) Can you explain PV, AC and EV?

PV (Planned Value): PV is also termed as (BCWS) Budgeted cost of work scheduled. It answers "How much do we plan to spend till this date?". It's the total budgeted cost for the project.

AC (Actual Cost): AC is also termed as ACWP (Actual cost of Work Scheduled). It answers "How much have we actually spent?".

EV (Earned Value): EV is also termed as BCWP (Budgeted Cost of Work Performed). It answers "How much work has actually been completed?".

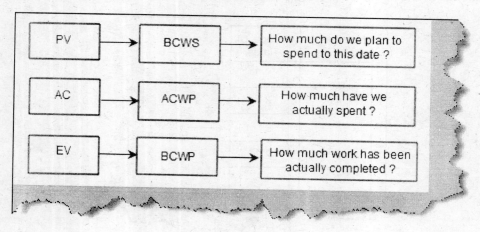

Figure: PV, AC and EV

Many project managers traditionally use only Actual and Planned values. But it's very much possible that you will not get proper results from the same. For instance consider the project shown in figure 'Actual and Planned'. The project duration is 5 weeks. According to the planned value graph in Week1 we will spend 600$, in week3 we will spend 3800 $ and on the completion of project it is 6000$.

But we where getting computers at a discounted cost in Week1 itself so we bought the computer. According to plan we are supposed to spend in Week1 750 $ but in actual we have spent 3000$. By comparing with the actual plan value we have concluded that we are over budget by 2250 $ in the first week. But that's not the actual case; in reality we bought the computers on discounted rate. So the graph is showing something really wrong. This issue is solved by using EV (Earned Value).

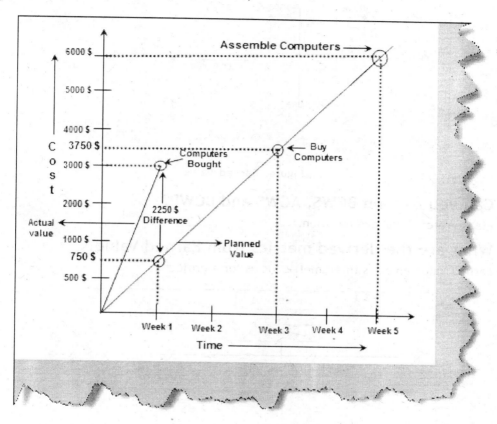

Figure: Actual and Planned

Earned Value measures progress and gives us forecasting, thus giving us an actual measure of the health of the project. For instance see the figure 'Earned Value'. We have given two views one is the planned value and the other is the earned value. According to the planned value it's a four week project with 25% (2500 $) work completed on Week1, 50 % (5000$) work completed on Week2 and so on. Now when the project starts executing on Week1 only 20% work is completed which means we have spent 2000$ and on week2 only 30 % work is completed. 2000$ and 3000$ shows the earned value for Week1 and Week2.

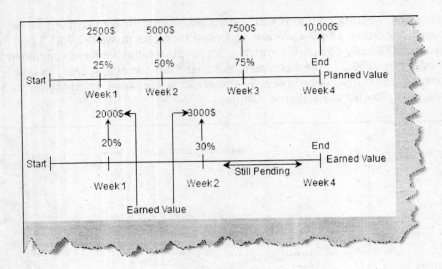

Figure: Earned Value

(B)   Can you explain BCWS, ACWS and BCWP?

Please refer the above question.

(B)   What are the derived metrics from Earned Value?

Earned Value gives us three metric views for a project.

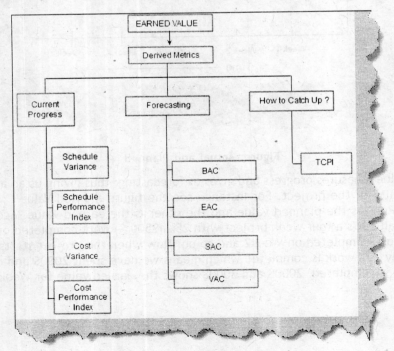

Figure: Earned Value Metrics

Current Progress: This shows how we are performing in the project.

Forecasting: Will help us answer how we will do in the project in future.

How will we catch up: In case the project is moving behind schedule or over budget how do we make up?

Current Progress metrics

Schedule Variance (SV)

Schedule variance is the difference between Earned value and planned value.

$$SV = EV - PV$$

SV	Description
0	You are on right schedule.
Negative	You are behind schedule.
Positive	You are ahead of schedule.

Cost Variance (CV)

Cost variance is the difference between earned value and the actual cost.

$$CV = EV - AC$$

CV	Description
0	You are on right on budget.
Negative	You are over budget.
Positive	You are under budget.

Cost performance Index (CPI)

CPI is the ratio of Earned value to Actual cost.

$$CPI = EV / AC$$

CPI	Description
1	You are right on budget.
Less than 1	You are over budget.
Greater than 1	You are under budget.

Schedule performance Index

SPI is the ratio of (Earned Value) EV to (Planned Value) PV.

$$SPI = EV / PV$$

SPI	Description
1	You are right on schedule.
Less than 1	You are behind schedule.
Greater than 1	You are ahead of schedule.

Forecasting

EVA helps us to also forecast our project schedule below is the metrics for the same.

Metric's Name	Description
Budget at completion (BAC)	This is the total original budgeted cost. It is same as the planned value.
Estimate at completion (EAC)	This is the final cost of the project. EAC = PV / CPI where PV is the planned value and CPI is the cost performance index.
Schedule at completion (SAC)	This represents the estimated duration of the project. SAC = Schedule / SPI Where schedule is the estimate schedule and SPI is the schedule performance index.
VAC (Variance at Completion)	It is the forecast of the final cost variance. VAC = BAC - EAC.

How will we catch up?

This is the third view which EV gives us. If the project is not on schedule how do we catch up with the same?. EV gives us something called as To-Complete performance Index (TCPI). TCPI is in an indication of how much we should perform to meet the project schedule.

$$TCPI = (\ Planned\ budget - EV\ )\ /\ (\ Final\ cost - AC\ )$$

TCPI	Description
Greater than 1	We need to perform better than the schedule.
Less than 1	We can reach the destination with schedule.

(A) Can you explain earned value with a sample?

Let's take a small sample project. We need to make 400 breads and following is the estimation of the project:-

·   We need to make 400 breads.

·   It will take 10 hours to make 400 breads.

·   Each bread will cost 0.02 $.

·   Total cost of making 400 breads is 400 X 0.02 = 8$.

·   In one hour we should be able to make 40 breads.

Below graph "Bread Project" shows the planned value and the actual cost graph. According to the planned value in 3 hours we will make 120 breads, in 7 hours we will make 280 breads and finally we will complete the 400 bread target in 10 hours. As the project moves ahead actually in the 3 rd hour we have only completed 80 breads with 3$ spent.

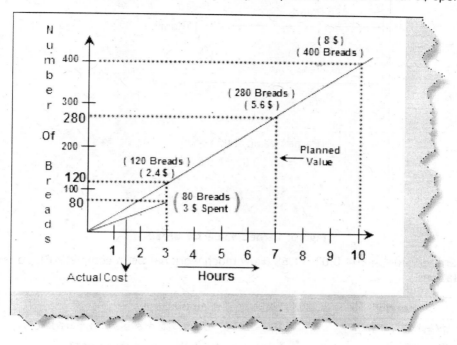

Figure: Bread Project

Ok, now that we know the actuals its time to calculate the EV, PV and the AC. In the 3ʳᵈ hour below is the analysis.

$$PV \text{ (Planned value)} = 120 * 0.02 = 2.4 \text{ \$.}$$

$$AC \text{ (Actual Cost)} = 3\$$$

Now it's the time to calculate the earned value. Below figure 'Earned Value for Bread' shows the simplified view of the bread project.

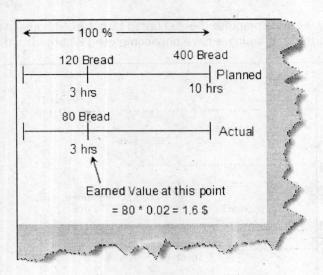

Figure: Earned Value for Bread

EV (Earned Value) = 80 * 0.02 = 1.6$ (How much work has been completed?). So let's do all calculations.

Metrics	Calculations
SV = EV - PV	1.6 - 2.4 = -0.8 (We are behind schedule)
CV = EV - AC	1.6 - 3 = -1.4 (We are over budget)
SPI = EV/PV	1.6/2.4 = 0.6 (We are behind schedule)
CPI = EV/AC	1.6/3 = 0.53 (We are over budget)
TCPI = (Planned - EV) / (Final - AC)	(8-1.6)/(8-3) = 1.28 i.e. (We have to perform 128 percent higher to reach our goal of making 400 breads in 10 hours)

5

Estimation, Metrics and Measure

(B) What is meant by measure and metrics?

Measures are quantitative unit defined elements for instance Hours, Km etc. Metrics comprises of more than one measure for instance, we can have metrics like Km/Hr, M/S etc.

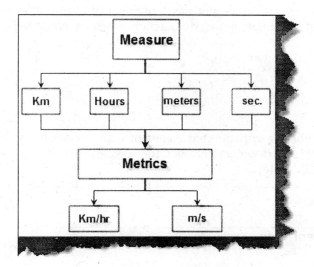

Figure: Measure and Metrics

(B) Which metrics have you used for tracking purpose?

This answer is subjective. Depending on the project a project manager decides which metric is good for his project. Mostly we have seen EV, AC and PV used across many projects.

> **Note:** *Please refer costing chapter to get in depth details of EV, AC and PV metrics.*

(B) What are the various common ways of estimation?

There are many ways of estimation in software industry. Frankly we can not really say which estimation methodology can be asked during interview. But let's concentrate on those estimation methodologies which are widely accepted. Below are some of the most used methodologies:

·   LOC (Lines of Code).

·   COCOMO.

·   Function Points.

·   Use case points.

·   SMC (Simple, Medium and Complex).

(B) Can you explain LOC method of estimation?

LOC (Lines of Code) is a metric to measure size of software program by counting the number of lines in the program's source code. There are two types of LOC units:

·   **Physical Lines of Code**: In physical lines of code means counting even comments, spaces, automated generated code etc.

·   **Logical Lines of Code**: In logical lines of code we only count the code which actually contributes towards running the program. For instance comments and spaces are not counted.

For instance the below code snippet has 5 physical lines of code while 2 logical lines of code (we excluded comments and curly brackets when we count logical lines of code).

```
// Loop and display the value
for (int i = 0; i < 10; i++)
{
    System.Console.WriteLine(Convert.ToString(i));
}
```

SEI (Software Engineering Institute) has come out with a check list called as 'Logical Source Statement of code'. So if we want to get the logical lines of code we should follow the below simplified SEI table.

Litmus Test	Include in Counting or Not
Depending on Statement Type	
Executable	Yes
Non-executable	
Declarations	Yes
Compiler directives	Yes

Comments	
On their Own lines	No
On lines with Source Code	No
Banners and nonblank spacers	No
Blank (Empty) Comments	No
Blank Lines	No
How Produced	
Programmed = =	Yes
Generated with Source Code Generators	Yes
Converted with automated Translators	Yes
Copied or reused without Change	Yes
Modified	Yes
Removed	No
Origin	
New Work: no Prior Existence	Yes
Prior Work: Taken or adapted from	
A previous version, build or release	Yes
COTS Commercial, off- the- shelf Software, other then reuse libraries	Yes
Another Product	Yes
A vendor- supplied language support library (unmodified)	No
A vendor- supplied Operating system or utility (unmodified)	No
A local or modified language support Library or operating System	Yes
Other Commercial library	Yes
A reuse library (software designed for reuse)	Yes
Other software component or library	Yes
Usage	
In or as part of primary product	Yes
External to or in support of the primary product	Yes
Delivery	
Delivered	
Delivered as Source	Yes
Delivered in Compiled or executable form, but not as source	Yes
Not delivered	
Under Configuration control	No
Not under configuration control	No
Functionality	

Operative	Yes
Inoperative (Dead, bypassed, unused, unreferenced or unaccessed)	
Functional (Intentional Dead Code, reactivated for special purpose)	Yes
Nonfunctional (unintentionally present)No	No
Replications	
Master Source Statements (originals)	Yes
Physical replicates of master statements, stored in master code	Yes
Copies inserted, instantiated, or expanded when compiling or linking	No
Postproduction replicates- as in distributed, redundant or reparameterized systems	No
Development status	
Estimated or planned	No
Designed	No
Coded	No
Unit tests Completed	No
Integrated into components	No
Test readiness review completed	No
Software (CI) test completed	No
System test completed	Yes

Table: SEI check list (Courtesy SEI)

If you count line of code with out using SEI check list that means it is physical lines of code.

Advantages of LOC

- Counting LOC is Simple.
- As they are final deliverables they can be used as Base Line to define companies' productivity.

Disadvantages of LOC

- Earlier estimation is difficult.
- Difficult to convince the end customer saying that project is 1000 lines of code so the cost is "XYZ" dollars.

(B) How do we convert LOC in to effort?

LOC finally needs to be converted to man days/man hours or man months. There are two ways either by using baseline technique or using COCOMO. In base line technique we have a company history which says that a developer for this language can delivery x amount of LOC so for this much LOC how much.

COCOMO is covered in depth in the coming questions.

(B) Can you explain COCOMO?

COCMO (Constructive Cost Model) is a parametric estimation model. It is not a size measurement methodology. On the contrary its takes in size and then applies non-functional characteristics of a project. When we say non-function characteristic we mean by:

· Is the team interaction good or bad?

· Are we using prototype model?

· Which software life cycle process are we following?

The above things can not be measured. So what COCOMO does is it take size as a parameter and applies these non-functional aspects of the project. In short it is a formula. The size input is LOC and the effort output is in man months. Below figure shows how COCOMO works. It takes LOC and gives the effort in man months.

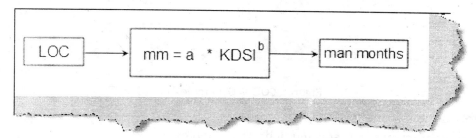

$$mm = a \ * \ KDSI^b$$

Figure: Basic COCOMO

Before we go in depth of the above formula, let's understand the principle on which COCOMO works. COCOMO says that any software has two aspects to be considered for estimation. One aspect is the complexity of the software and the other project development mode.

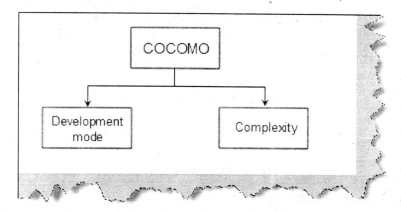

Figure: COCOMO Estimation view

Complexity Aspect

COCOMO views two types of complexity in a software project, one is the multiplicative complexity and the other is the exponential complexity. Exponential complexities of a project are those aspects, if they change slightly the estimation changes in a very huge manner. Multiplicative complexities are those aspects if they change only a proportional changes happen to estimation. For instance a changing customer issue is an exponential factor while a new technology is a multiplicative factor.

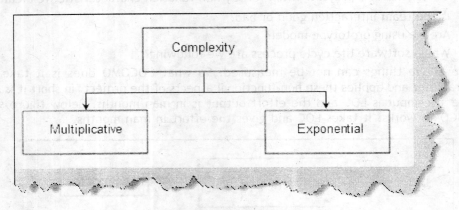

Figure: COCOMO Complexity

Below is the formula for COCOMO.

a: This coefficient represents multiplicative complexity.

b: This coefficient represents exponential complexity.

KDSI: KDSI is the delivered source instruction. In short they are physical lines of code.

MM: Man month i.e. one month of effort by one person or one staff.

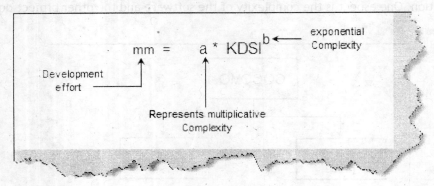

Figure: COCOMO Formulae

Project development mode

The above two coefficients 'a' and 'b' depends on project development mode. Below figure 'Development mode table' shows the different development mode. There are basically three development modes which are decided on basis of size, innovation, how is the deadline and the development environment. Depending on the same we have given values for 'a' and 'b'. There is one more coefficient introduced 'c' which will be used to calculate development time.

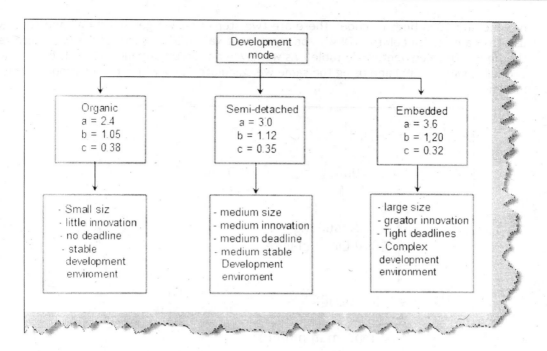

Figure: Development mode table

To calculate development time below is the formulae. So from the first formula we need to calculate the MM (man month) which is then fed in the below formula effort and development time.

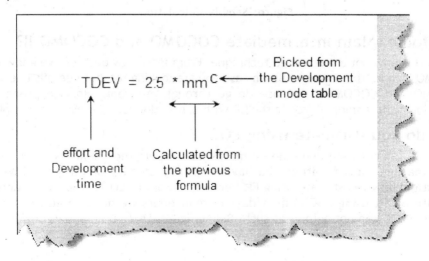

Figure: Effort and Development time

Let's try to understand COCOMO with small sample. Below figure 'Sample Calculation' explains the same in a more detailed manner. We have considered development mode as organic and 1000 lines of code. There are two steps first we get the "MM" and then we use the same to calculate 'TDEV'. For coefficient value 'a','b' and 'c' we have referred the figure 'Development mode table'. As we have considered organic so a=2.4, b=1.05 and c=0.38. So MM is 3390 and using the same we calculate TDEV which comes around 54 man months.

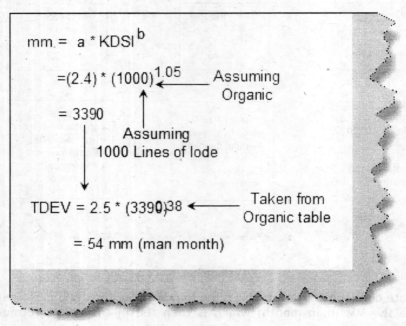

Figure: Sample Calculation

(I) Can you explain Intermediate COCOMO and COCOMO II?

COCOMO is now not a much used technique. From interview perspective knowing the basic COCOMO is more than enough. But in case you are looking for more details like intermediate COCOMO and COCOMO II, please do go through my book 'How to prepare Software Quotations?'. It is shipped free in the CD with name 'HowtoPrepareSoftwareQuotations.pdf'.

(B) How do you estimate using LOC?

In LOC we can not determine the estimates just by pure requirements. There are two ways of estimating. First is either you have a history of data or either FP. We will try to understand how to estimate using FP, because history of LOC can be very inconsistent. To estimate effort using LOC in man/days or man/hours we need to also use COCOMO and FP. Alone LOC can not help us as such. Below figure 'Using LOC' shows how we can get the effort.

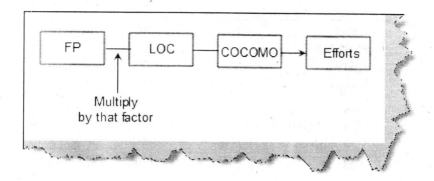

Figure: Using LOC

Step 1: We estimate using function points and get the number of function points (In the further chapters we have given the full details of how FP counting works).

Step 2: If you have history of how many FP is how many lines of code use your company history or else you can refer the below table which has been collected from QSM database. There are many standard databases available which can give you the conversion. From this you will know how many LOC will be derived for that particular FP.

Step 3: Feed the derived LOC in to the COCOMO formula which was explained previously and you will get the results in man/months.

Below table is taken from Source http://www.qsm.com/FPGearing.html

Language	SLOC / FP
Access	38
ADA	-
Advantage	38
APS	83
ASP	62
Assembler**	157
C **	104
C++ **	53
C#	59
Clipper	39
COBOL **	77
Cool:Gen/IEF	31
Culprit	-
DBase III	-
DBase IV	-
Easytrieve+	34
Excel	46

Focus	42
FORTRAN	-
FoxPro	35
HTML**	42
Ideal	52
IEF/Cool:Gen	31
Informix	31
J2EE	50
Java**	59
JavaScript**	54
JCL**	48
JSP	
Lotus Notes	22
Mantis	27
Mapper	81
Natural	52
Oracle**	29
Oracle Dev 2K/FORMS	30
Pacbase	48
PeopleSoft	32
Perl	-
PL/1**	58
PL/SQL	31
Powerbuilder**	24
REXX	-
RPG II/III	49
Sabretalk	89
SAS	41
Siebel Tools	13
Slogan	82
Smalltalk**	32
SQL**	35
VBScript**	34
Visual Basic**	42
VPF	95
Web Scripts	15

Table: QSM database

Let's do a simple sample estimation using LOC. Below are the assumptions for the project.

Assumptions	
Function points	400
Language	C#
Development mode	Organic

Table: Assumptions for COCOMO

Below figure 'LOC calculation' shows the effort calculation using LOC. Basically there are three steps:

· We convert function points in to LOC using the QSM database. You can see how to do function point counting in the further questions. So according to the assumption function point value is 400 and from the QSM database the C# LOC for one FP is 59. So LOC is 23600 lines of code.

· Assuming that the development mode is organic so a = 2.4 and b=1.05. Man month effort comes to 93706.

· Using the man month effort we calculate TDEV. As its organic the value of c = 0.38. The final calculation comes to 193 man month.

Below diagram shows the above calculation in a phase wise manner.

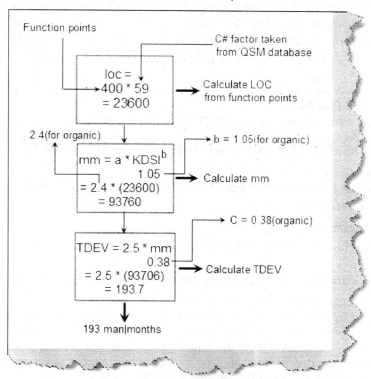

Figure: LOC calculation

(A) Can you explain in brief Function points?

> **Note:**   *It's rare that some one will ask you to say full details of function points*
> *in one shot. They will rather ask specific sections like GSC, ILF etc. The*
> *main interest of the interviewer will do you have a broader idea of*
> *estimating using function points.*

Introduction to Function Points

> *"This document contains material which has been extracted from the IFPUG*
> *Counting Practices Manual. It is reproduced in this document with the*
> *permission of IFPUG."*

Function Point Analysis was developed first by Allan J. Albrecht in the mid 1970s. It was an attempt to overcome difficulties associated with lines of code as a measure of software size, and to assist in developing a mechanism to predict effort associated with software development. The method was first published in 1979, then later in 1983. In 1984 Albrecht refined the method and since 1986, when the International Function Point User Group (IFPUG) was set up, several versions of the Function Point Counting Practices Manual have been coming out.

> *"The best way to understand any complicated system is breaking the system in*
> *to smaller subsystem and try to understand those smaller sub-systems . In*
> *Function Point you break complicated huge system into smaller systems and*
> *estimate those smaller pieces, then total up all the subsystem estimate to come*
> *up with final estimate."*

Basics of Function Points

Following are some terms used in FPA [Function Point analysis].

(B) Can you explain the concept Application boundary?

Application Boundary

The first step in FPA is defining boundary. There are two types of major boundaries:

- Internal Application Boundary
- External Application Boundary

We will state features of external application boundary, so that internal application boundary would be self explained.

External Application Boundary can be identified using following litmus test:

- Does it have or will have any other interface to maintain its data, which is not Developed by you. Example: Your Company is developing an "Accounts Application" and at the end of accounting year, you have to report to tax Department. Tax department has his own website where companies can connect and report there Tax transaction. Tax department application has other Maintenance and reporting screens been developed by tax software department.   These maintenance screens are used internally by the Tax department. So Tax Online interface has other interface to maintain its data which is not your scope, thus we can identify Tax website reporting as External Application.

· Does your program have to go through a third party API or layer? In order your application interacts with Tax Department Application probably your code have to interact through Tax Department API.

· The best litmus test is to ask yourself do you have full access over the system. If you have full rights or command to change then its internal application boundary or else external application boundary.

(B) Can you explain the concept of elementary process?

(B) Can you explain the concept of static and dynamic elementary process?

Elementary Process

As said in introduction FPA is breaking huge systems in to smaller pieces and analyzing them. Software application is combination of set of elementary processes.

> *EP is smallest unit of activity that is meaningful to the user. EP must be self contained and leave the application in a consistent state.*

When elementary processes come together they form a software application.

> **Note:** *Elementary process is not necessarily completely independent or can exist by itself.So, we can define elementary process as small units of self contained functionality from user perspective.*

Dynamic and static elementary process

There are two types of elementary process:

· Dynamic Elementary process.
· Static Elementary process.

Dynamic elementary process moves data from internal application boundary to external Application boundary or vice-versa.

Examples of dynamic elementary process:

· Input data screen where user inputs data in to application. Data moves from the input screen inside application.

· Transaction exported in export files in XML or any other standard.

· Display reports which can come from external application boundary and internal application boundary.

Examples of static elementary process:

· Static elementary process maintains data of application either inside application boundary or in external application boundary.

For instance in a customer maintenance screen maintaining customer data is static elementary process.

(I) Can you explain concept of FTR, ILF, EIF, EI, EO, EQ and GSC ?

Elements of Function Points

Following are the elements of FPA.

Internal Logical Files (ILF)

Following are points to be noted for ILF:

- ILF are logically related data from user point of view.
- They reside in Internal Application boundary and are maintained through Elementary process of application.
- ILF can have maintenance screen or probably not.

> **Caution:** *Do not make a mistake of mapping one to one relationship between ILF and technical database design, then FPA can go very misleading. The main difference between ILF and technical database is ILF is logical view and database is physical structure (Technical Design). Example Supplier database design will have tables like Supplier, Supplier Address, SupplierPhonenumbers, but from ILF point of view its only Supplier. As logically they are all Supplier details.*

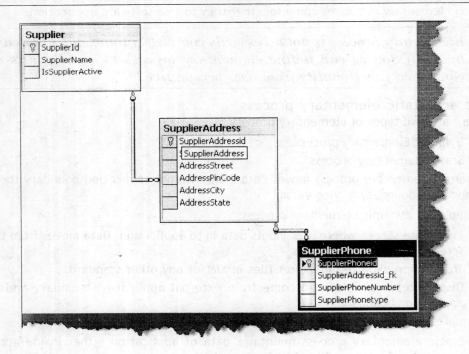

Figure: ILF example

External Interface File (EIF)

- They are logically related data from user point of view.

- EIF reside in external application boundary.
- EIF is used only for reference purpose and are not maintained by internal application.
- EIF is maintained by external application.

Record Element Type (RET)

Following are points to be noted for RET

- RET are sub-group element data of ILF or EIF.
- If there is no sub-group of ILF then count the ILF itself as one RET.
- A group of RET's within ILF are logically related. Most probably with a parent child relationship. Example: Supplier had multiple addresses and every address can have multiple phone numbers (See detail image below which shows database diagrams).So Supplier, Supplier Address and Supplier phone numbers are RET's.

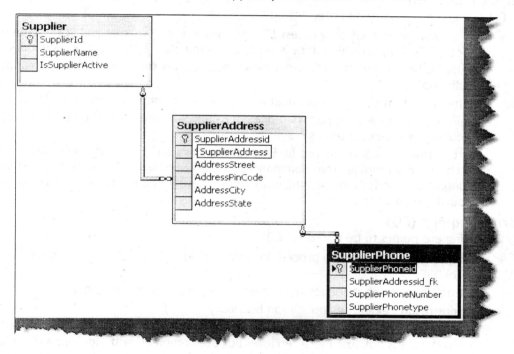

Figure: RET

Please note the whole database is one supplier ILF as all belong to one logical section. RET quantifies the relationship complexity of ILF and EIF.

DET (Data element types)

Following are the points to be noted for DET counting:

- Each DET should be User recognizable. Example in the above given figure we have kept auto increment field (Supplierid) for primary key. Supplierid field from user point of view never exists at all, its only from software designing aspect, so does not qualifies for DET.
- DET should be non-recursive field in ILF. DET should not repeat in the same ILF again,

it should be counted only once.

· Count foreign keys as one DET. "Supplierid" does not qualifies as DET but its relationship in "supplieraddress" table is counted as DET. So "Supplierid_fk" in supplieraddress table is counted as DET. Same folds true for "Supplieraddressid_fk".

File Type Reference (FTR)

Following are points to be noted for FTR:

· FTR is files or data referenced by a transaction.

· FTR should be ILF or EIF. So count each ILF or EIF read during process.

· If the EP is maintaining an ILF then count that as FTR. So by default you will always have one FTR in any EP.

External Input (EI)

Following are points to be noted for EI:

· It's a dynamic elementary process [For definition see "Dynamic and Static Elementary Process" Section] in which data is received from external application boundary.

  Example: User Interaction Screens, when data comes from User Interface to Internal Application.

· EI may maintain ILF of the application, but it's not compulsory rule.

  Example: A calculator application does not maintain any data, but still the screen of calculator will be counted as EI.

· Most of time User Screens will be EI, again no hard and fast rule. Example: An import batch process running from command line does not have screen, but still should be counted as EI as it helps passing data from External Application Boundary to Internal Application Boundary.

External Inquiry (EQ)

Following are points to be noted for EQ:

· It's a dynamic elementary process in which result data is retrieved from one or more ILF or EIF.

· In this EP some input request has to enter the application boundary.

· Output results exits the application boundary.

· EQ does not contain any derived data. Derived data means any complex calculated data. Derived data is not just mere retrieval but are combined with additional formulae to generate results. Derived data is not part of ILF or EIF, they are generated on fly.

· EQ does not update any ILF or EIF.

· EQ activity should be meaningful from user perspective.

· EP is self contained and leaves the business in consistent state.

· DET and processing logic is different from other EQ's.

· Simple reports form good base as EQ.

> **Note:** *No hard and fast rules that only simple reports are EQ's. Simple view functionality can also be counted as EQ.*

External Output (EO)

Following are points to be noted for EO:

- It's a dynamic elementary process in which derived data crosses from Internal Application Boundary to External Application Boundary.
- EO can update an ILF or EIF.
- Process should be the smallest unit of activity that is meaningful to end userin business.
- EP is self contained and leaves the business in a consistent state.
- DET is different from other EO's.So this ensures to us that we do not count EO's twice.
- They have derived data or formulae calculated data.

Major difference between EO and EQ is that data passes across application boundary.

Example: Exporting Accounts transaction to some external file format like XML or some other format. Which later the external accounting software can import. Second important difference is in EQ its non-derived data and EO has derived data.

General System Characteristic Section (GSC)

This section is the most important section. All the above discussed sections are counting sections. They relate only to application. But there are other things also to be considered while making software, like are you going to make it an N-Tier application, what's the performance level the user is expecting etc these other factors are called GSC. These are external factors which affect the software a lot and also the cost of it. When you submit a function point to a client, he normally will skip everything and come to GSC first. GSC gives us something called as VAF (Value Added Factor).

There are 14 points considered to come out with VAF (Value Added factor) and its associated rating table.

Data Communications

How many communication facilities are there to aid in the transfer or exchange of information with the application or system?

Rating	Description
0	Application is pure batch processing or a standalone PC.
1	Application is batch but has remote data entry or remote Printing.
2	Application is batch but has remote data entry and remote Printing.
3	Application includes online data collection or TP (Teleprocessing) front end to a batch process or query system.
4	Application is more than a front-end, but supports only one Type of TP communications protocol.
5	Application is more than a front-end, and supports more than One type of TP communications protocol.

Table: Data Communication

Distributed data processing

How are distributed data and processing functions handled?

Rating	Description
0	Application does not aid the transfer of data or processing Function between components of the system.
1	Application prepares data for end user processing on another component of the system such as PC spreadsheets and PC DBMS
2	Data is prepared for transfer, then is transferred and processed on another component of the system (not for end-user Processing).
3	Distributed processing and data transfer are online and in One direction only.
4	Distributed processing and data transfer are online and in Both directions.
5	Processing functions are dynamically performed on the most Appropriate component of the system

Table: Distributed data processing

Performance

Did the user require response time or throughput?

Rating	Description
0	No special performance requirements were stated by the User.
1	Performance and design requirements were stated and Reviewed but no special actions were required.
2	Responsetimeorthroughputiscriticalduringpeakhours.NospecialdesignforCPU utilization was required. Processing deadline is for the next business day.
3	Response time or through put is critical during all business hours. No special design for CPU utilizationwasrequired.Processingdeadlinerequirementswithinterfacing systems Are constraining.
4	In addition, stated user performance requirements are stringent enough to require performance analysis tasks in the Design phase.
5	In addition, performance analysis tools were used in the design, development, and/or implementation phases to meet The stated user performance requirements.

Table: Performance

Heavily used configuration

How heavily used is the current hardware platform where the application will be executed?

Rating	Description
0	No explicit or implicit operational restrictions are included.
1	Operational restrictions do exist, but are less restrictive than a typical application. No special effort is needed to meet the Restrictions.
2	Some security or timing considerations are included.
3	Specific processor requirement for a specific piece of the Application is included.
4	Stated operation restrictions require special constraints on the application in the central processor or a dedicated Processor.
5	In addition, there are special constraints on the application in The distributed components of the system.

Table: **Heavily used configuration**

Transaction rate

How frequently are transactions executed; daily, weekly, monthly, etc.?

Rating	Description
0	No peak transaction period is anticipated.
1	Peak transaction period (e.g., monthly, quarterly, seasonally, Annually) is anticipated.
2	Weekly peak transaction period is anticipated.
3	Daily peak transaction period is anticipated.
4	High transaction rate(s) stated by the user in the application requirements or service level agreements are high enough to Require perform ance analysis tasks in the design phase.
5	High transaction rate(s) stated by the user in the application requirem ents or service level agreements are high enough to require performance analysis tasks and, in addition, require the use of performance analysis tools in the design, Development, and/or installation phases.

Table: **Transaction rate**

On-Line data entry

What percentage of the information is entered On-Line?

Rating	Description
0	All transactions are processed in batch mode.
1	1% to7% of transactions is interactive data entry.
2	8% to15% of transactions is interactive data entry.
3	16% to23% of transactions is interactive data entry.
4	24% to30% of transactions is interactive data entry.
5	M orethan30% of transactions is interactive data entry.

Table: **Online data entry**

End-user efficiency

Was the application designed for end-user efficiency? There are seven end-user efficiency factors which govern how this point is rated.

Sr no	End-user Efficiency Factor
1	Navigational aids(for example, function keys, jumps, dynamically generated menus)
2	Menus
3	Online help and documents
4	Automated curs or movement
5	Scrolling
6	Remote printing(via online transactions)
7	Preassigned function keys
8	Batch jobs submitted from online transactions
9	Cursor selection of screen data
10	Heavy use of reverse video, highlighting, colors underlining, and other indicators
11	Hard copy user documentation of online transactions
12	Mouse interface
13	Pop-up windows
14	.As few screens as possible to accomplish a business function
15	Bilingual support(supports two languages; count as four items)
16	Multilingual support (supports more than two languages; count as six items).

Table: End user efficiency factor

Rating	Description
0	None of the above.
1	One to three of the above.
2	Four to five of the above.
3	Six or more of the above, but there are no specific user Requirements related to efficiency.
4	Six or more of the above, and stated requirements for end-user efficiency are strong enough to require design tasks for human factors to be included (for example, minimize keystrokes, maximize defaults, use of templates).
5	Six or more of the above, and stated requirements for end-user efficiency are strong enough to require use of special tools and processes to demonstrate that the objectives have been achieved.

Table: End user efficiency

On-Line update

How many ILF's are updated by On-Line transaction?

Rating	Description
0	None of the above.
1	Online update of one to three control files is included. Volume of updating I slow and recovery is easy.
2	Online update off our or more control files is included. Volume of updating is low and recovery easy.
3	Online update of major internal logical files is included.
4	In addition, protection against data lost is essential and has been specially designed and programmed in the system.
5	In addition, high volumes bring cost considerations into the Recovery process. Highly automated recovery procedures With minimum operator intervention are included.

Table: Online update

Complex processing

Does the application have extensive logical or mathematical processing?

Sr no	Complex Processing Factor
1	Sensitive control(for example, special audit processing)and/or application specific security Processing
2	Extensive logical processing
3	Extensive mathematical processing
4	Much exception processing resulting in incomplete transactions that must be processed again, for example, incomplete ATM transactions caused by TP interruption, missing data values, or failed edits
5	Complex processing to handle multiple input/output possibilities, for example, multimedia, or device independence

Table: Complex processing factor

Rating	Description
0	None of the above.
1	Any one of the above.
2	Any two of the above.
3	Any three of the above.
4	Any four of the above.
5	All five of the above

Table: Complex processing

Reusability

Was the application developed to meet one or many user's needs?

Rating	Description
0	No reusable code.
1	Reusable code is used within the application.
2	Less than 10% of the application considered more than one user's needs.
3	Ten percent (10%) or more of the application considered more than one user's needs.
4	The application was specifically packaged and/or documented to ease re-use, and the application is customized by the user at source code level.
5	The application was specifically packaged and/or documented to ease re-use, and the application is customized for use by means of user parameter maintenance.

Table: reusability

Installation ease

How difficult is conversion and installation

Rating	Description
0	No special considerations were stated by the user, and no special setup is required for installation.
1	No special considerations were stated by the user but special setup is required for installation.
2	Conversion and installation requirements were stated by the user and conversion and installation guides were provided and tested. The impact of conversion on the project is not considered to be important.
3	Conversion and installation requirements were stated by the user, and conversion and installation guides were provided And tested. The impact of conversion on the project is Considered to be important.
4	In addition to 2 above, automated conversion and installation Tools were provided and tested.
5	In addition to 3 above, automated conversion and installation Tools were provided and tested.

Table: Installation ease

Operational ease

How effective and/or automated are start-up, back up, and recovery procedures?

Rating	Description
0	No special operational considerations so other than the normal Back- up procedures were stated by the user.
1-4	One, some, or all of the following items apply to the Application. Select all that apply. Each item has a point Value of one, except as noted otherwise.
	Effective start-up, back-up, and recovery processes were Provided, but operator intervention is required.
	Effective start-up, back-up, and recovery processes were provided, but no operator intervention is required(count as Two items).
	The application minimizes the need for tape mounts.
	The application minimizes the need for paper handling.
5	The application is designed for unattended operation. Unattended operation means no operator intervention is required to operate the system other than to startup or shutdown the application.Automatic error recovery is a feature Of the application.

Table: operational ease

Multiple sites

Was the application specifically designed, developed, and supported to be installed at multiple sites for multiple organizations?

Rating	Description
0	User requirements do not require considering the needs of More than one user/installation site.
1	Needs of multiple sites were considered in the design, and the application is designed to operate only under identical Hardware and software environments.
2	Needs of multiple sites were considered in the design, and the application is designed to operate only under similar Hardware and or software environments.
3	Needs of multiple sites were considered in the design, and the application is designed to operate under different Hardware and or software environments.
4	Documentation and support plan are provided and tested to support the application at multiple sites and the application is as described by 1 or 2.
5	Documentation and support plan are provided and tested to support the application at multiple sites and the application is as described by 3.

Table: Multiple sites

Facilitate change

Was the application specifically designed, developed, and supported to facilitate change?.

The following characteristics can apply for the application

Sr no	Facilitate factors
0	None of above
1	Flexible query and report facility is provided that can handle simple requests; for example, and/or logic applied to only one internal logical file (count as one item).
2	Flexible query and report facility is provided that can handle requests of average complexity for example, and/or logic applied to more than one internal logical file (count as two items).
3	Flexible query and report facility is provided that can handle complex requests, for example, and/or logic combinations on one or more internal logical files (count as three items).
4	Business control data is kept in tables that are maintained by the user with online interactive Processes, but changes take effect only on the next business day.
5	Business control data is kept in tables that are maintained by the user with online interactive Processes and the changes take effect immediately (count as two items)

Table: Facilitate change factors

Rating	Description
0	None of the above.
1	Any one of the above.
2	Any two of the above.
3	Any three of the above.
4	Any four of the above.
5	All five of the above

Table: Facilitate change

All the above GSC are rated from 0-5. Then VAF is calculated from the equation below:

VAF = 0.65 + ((sum of all GSC factor)/100).

> *Note:* GSC has not been accepted in software industry widely. Many software companies use Unadjusted Function point rather than adjusted. ISO has also removed GSC from its books and only kept unadjusted function points as the base for measurement. Read GSC acceptance in software industry Rating Tables for All elements of Function Points.

Below shown are look up tables which will be referred during counting.

EI Rating Table			
Data Elements			
FTR	1 to 4	5 to 15	Greater than 15
Less than 2	3	3	4
Equal to 23	4	6	
Greater than 2	4	4	6

Table: EI rating table

This table says that in any EI (External Input), if your DET count (Data Element) and FTR (File Type Reference) exceed these limits, then this should be the FP (Function Point). Example, if your DET (data element) exceeds >15 and FTR (File Type Reference) is greater than 2, then the Function Point count is 6. The rest down tables also show the same things. These tables will be there before us when we are doing function point count. The best is put these values in Excel with formulae so that you have to only put quantity in the appropriate section and you get the final value.

EO Rating Table			
Data Elements			
FTR	1 to 5	6 to 19	Greater than 19
Less than 2	4	4	5
2 or 3	4	5	7
Greater than 2	5	7	7

Table: EO rating table

EQ Rating Table			
Data Elements			
FTR	1 to 5	6 to 19	Greater than 19
Less than 2	3	3	4
2 or 3	3	4	6
Greater than 2	4	6	6

Table: EQ rating table

ILF Rating Table			
Data Elements			
RET	1 to 19	20 to 50	51 or more
1 RET	7	7	10
2 to 5	7	10	15
Greater than 6	10	15	15

EIF Rating Table			
RET	**1 to 19**	**20 to 50**	**51 or more**
1 RET	5	5	7
2 to 5	5	7	10
Greater than	6	7	10 10

Table: ILF rating table.

Steps to Count Function Points

This section will discuss the practical way of counting the FP and coming out with aMan/Days on a project.

- Counting the ILF, EIF, EI, EQ, RET, DET, FTR (this is basically all sections discussed above): This whole FP count will be called as "unadjusted function point".
- Then put rating values 0 to 5 to all 14 GSC. Adding total of all 14 GSC to come out with total VAF. Formula for VAF = 0.65 + (sum of all GSC factor/ 100).
- Finally, make the calculation of adjusted function point. Formula: Total function point = VAF * Unadjusted function point.
- Make estimation how many function points you will do per day. This is also called as "Performance factor".
- On basis of performance factor, you can calculate Man/Days]

Let's try to implement these details in a sample customer project.

Sample Customer Project

We will be evaluating the customer GUI. So we will just scope what the customer GUI is all about.

Following is the scope of the customer screen:

- Customer screen will be as shown below.
- After putting the customer code and Customer name. They will be verified credit card check.
- Credit Card check is a external system.
- Every Customer can have multiple addresses.
- Customer will have add, update functionality.

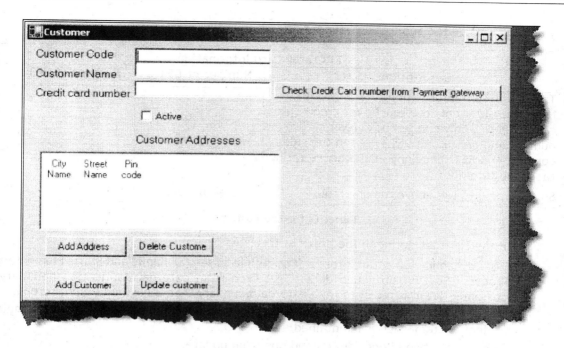

Figure: Custom screen

There is one ILF in the above screen:

·   The customer ILF.

There is one EIF in the above form.

·   Credit Card System

Following the ILF counting rules

·   ILF are logically related data from user point of view. Customer and Customer addresses belong logically to customer category.

·   ILF reside in Internal Application boundary and are maintained through Elementary process of application. Customer resides in inside application boundary as we have full access over it.

So hence goes the counting below for ILF

ILF Customer		
Description	**Number of DET**	**Number of RET**
There are total 9 DETs, alladd and update buttons, even the credit check button, the address list box, check box active, all text boxes. There is only one RET, the customer addresses.	9	1
So according to the above ILF ranking table	**Total function**	**7**

Table: ILF for the customer

EIF lie outside the application boundary.

EI Credit Card Information		
Description	Number of DET	Number of RET
The credit card information referenced is EIF. Note this file is only referenced for credit card check. There's only one textbox credit card number and hence one DET is put in the side column. And RET 0. Looking at the above rating table the total FP is 5.	1	1
So according to the above ranking table	Total function	5

Table: EI for the customer

Following EIF rules define in the previous sections:

- It's a dynamic elementary process [For definition see "Dynamic and Static Elementary Process" Section] in which data is received from external application boundary. Customer detail is received from external boundary that is customer input screen.
- EI may maintain ILF of the application, but it's not compulsory rule. In this sample project Customer ILF is maintained.
- So there are two EI one for Add and one from update.

It is two because processing logic for add and update is different.

EI Add Customer		
Description	Number of DET	Number of FTR
There are total 9 DETs, all add and update buttons, even the credit check button, the address list box, check box active, all text boxes. There are 3 FTRs, one is the address and the second is the credit card information and third is customer himself.	9	3
So according to the above ranking table	Total function	6

Table: EI for the add customer

EI Update Customer		
Description	Number of DET	Number of RET
There are total 9 DETs, all add and update buttons, even the credit check button, the address list box, check box active, all text boxes. There are 3 FTRs, one is the address and the second is the credit card information and third is customer himself.	9	3
So according to the above ranking table	Total function	6

Table: EI for the update customer

While counting EI I have seen many people multiplying it by 3. That means we are going to do all CRUD functionality (ADD, UPDATE, and DELETE). This is not fair as it just shows laziness of the Cost estimation team. Here the customer screen has add and update. I can say the 2 * 6 that's = 12 FP for this EI customer. But later when some refers to your FP sheet he will be completely lost.

Following are rules to recognize EO:

· Data should cross application boundary and it should involve complex logic.

Credit card check process can be complex as the credit card API complexity is still not known. Data that is credit card information crosses from credit card system to Customer system.

EO check credit card		
Description	Number of DET	Number of RET
One DET Credit Card number and one RET credit card itself. Note if there are no RET we count default as one. Look for RET counting rules defined in previous section.	1	1
So according to the above ranking table	Total function	4

Table: EO to check the credit card

Following are rules to recognize EQ:

· It's a dynamic elementary process in which result data is retrieved from one or more ILF or EIF. For editing the customer we will need to retrieve the customer details.

· In this EP some input request has to enter the application boundary. The customer code is inputted from the same screen.

· Output results exits the application boundary. The customer details is displayed while the customer is editing the customer data.

· EQ does not contain any derived data. The above customer data which is displayed does not contain any complex calculations.

EQ Display Customer Edit Information		
Description	Number of DET	Number of FTR
There are 5 DETs to be retrieved Customer Code, Customer Name, Credit Card number, Active, Customer Address. Only customer details and customer address will be referenced.	5	2
So according to the above ranking table	Total function	3

Table: EQ to display customer edit

So now, let's add the total function point got from above tables:

Function Point	Section Name Counted
ILF Customer	
EO Credit Card check system	4
EIF credit card information	5
EI Customer (Add and update)	12
EQ display customer edit information	3
Total UnadjustedFunction Points	31

Table: Total of all function point

So unadjusted function point comes to 31. Please note I have said this as Unadjusted function as we have not accounted other variance factor of project (Programmers leaving job, Language we will use, what architecture etc etc).

In order to make it adjusted function point, we have to calculate and tabulate the GSC and come out with the VAF.

GSC	Value(0-5)
Data communications	1
Distributed data processing	1
Performance 4	
Heavily used configuration	0
Transaction rate	1
On-Line data entry	0
End-user efficiency	4
On-Line update	0
Complex processing	0
Reusability 3	
Installation ease	4
Operational ease	4
Multiple sites	0
Facilitate change	0
Total	22

Table: GSC

$$VAF = 0.65 + ((sum\ of\ all\ GSC\ factor) / 100). = 0.65 + (22 / 100) = 0.87.$$

This factor affects the whole FP like anything, be very particular with this factor. So now, calculating the Adjusted FP = VAF * Total unadjusted

$$FP = 0.87 * 31 = 26.97 = rounded\ to\ 27\ FP.$$

Now we know that the complete FP for the customer GUI is 27 FP. Now calculating theefficiency factor, we say that we will complete 3 FP per day that is 9 working days. So, the whole customer GUI is of 9 working days (Note do not consider Saturday and Sundays in this). I know upper manager people will say make it 7 FP per day and over load the programmer. That's why programmer works at night.

Considering SDLC (System Development Life Cycle)

Before reading this section please refer to different SDLC cycles questions in the previous chapters.

The main intention of introducing this section is because quotations are heavily affectedby which software life cycle you follow. Because deliverables change according to SLDCmodel the project manager chooses for the project. Example for waterfall model we willhave Requirement documents, Design documents, Source code and testing plans. But forprototyping models in addition to the documents above we will also need to deliver therough prototype. For build and fix model we will not deliver any of the documents andthe only document delivered will be source code. So according to SDLC model deliverables change and hence the quotation. We will divide the estimation across requirement, design, implementation (coding) and testing .In what way the estimation has to divide across all deliverables is all up to the project manager and his plans.

Phase	Percentage distribution effort
Requirements	10% of total effort
Design Phase	20% of total effort
Coding	100 % of total effort
Testing	10% of total effort

Table: Phase wise distribution of effort

The above sample is total 100 % distribution of effort across various phases. But note function point or any other estimation methodology only gives you total execution estimation. So you can see in the above distribution we have given coding as 100 %. But as said it up to the project manager to change according to scenarios .Ok now from the above function point estimation the estimation is 7 days let's try to divide it across all phases.

Phase	Percentage distribution effort	Distribution of man/days across phases
Requirements	10 % of total effort	0.9 days
Design Phase	20 % of total effort	1.8 days
Coding	60 % of total effort	7 days .
Testing	10 % of total effort	0.9 days
Total	9 day	10.6 days

Table: Phase wise effort distribution of man days

The above table shows the division of project man/days across project. Now let's put down the final quotation. Just a small comment about test cases.

Total number of Test Cases = (Function Point) raised to power of 1.2. This is as suggested from caper Jones.

(A) How can you estimate number of acceptance test cases in a project?

> *Number of Acceptance Test Cases = 1.2 * Function Points*

20-25 % of total effort can be allocated to testing phase. Test cases are non-deterministic. That means if test passes it takes "X" amount of time and if it does not then to amend it take "Y" amount of time.

Final Quotation

One programmer will sit on the project with around 1000 $ salary / Month. So his 10.6 days salary comes to 341 dollars approx. The upper quotation format is in its simplest format. Every company has his quotation format accordingly. So no hard and fast rule of quotation template. But still if interested http://www.microsoft.com/mac/resources/templates.aspx?pid=templates has good collection of decent templates.

XYZ SOFTWARE COMPANY				
To: TNC Limited, Western road 17, California.Quotation number: 90Date: 1/1/ 2004 Customer ID: Z- 20090DATAENTRY				
Quantity	Description	Discount	Taxable	Total
1	Customer Project	0%	0%	41 dollars
Quotation Valid for 100 daysGoods delivery date with in 25 days of half paymentQuotation Prepared by: XYZ estimation departmentApproved by: SPEG department XYZ.				

Table - Final bill

CustomerSampleFP.xls is provided with the CD which has all estimation details whichyou can refer for practical approach.

GSC Acceptance in Software industry

GSC factors have been always a controversial topic. Most of the software companies do not use GSC, rather than they base line UAFP or construct there own table depending oncompany project history. ISO has also adopted function point as unit of measurement, but they also use UAFP rather than AFP. Let's do a small experiment to view relationship between FP, AFP, GSC and VAF. In this experiment we will assume UAFP = 120 and then lot graph with GSC increment of five. So the formulae is VAF = 0.65 + (GS/100).

Here's the table with every five incremental values in formulae and plot.

FP	GSC
78	0
84	5
90	10
96	15
102	20
108	25
114	30
120	35
126	40
132	45
138	50
144	55
150	60
156	65
162	70

Table: GSC acceptance

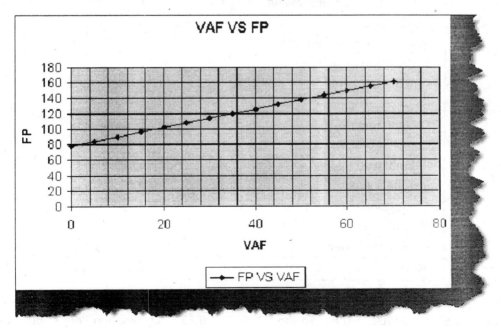

Figure: FP versus VAF

The following are the observation from the table and plot:

- Graph is linear. It also captures that nature of complexity is linear.
- If the GSC value is zero then VAF is 0.65. So the graph starts from UAFP*0.65.GSC = 35 AFP = UAFP. So the VAF = 1.
- When GSC < 35 then AFP < UAFP. That means complexity decreases.
- When GSC > 35 then AFP > UAFP. That means complexity increases.

Readers must be wondering why 0.65? There are fourteen GSC factor from zero to five. So the maximum value of VAF = 0.65 + (70/100) = 1.35. In order that VAF does not have any affect i.e. UAFP = FP VAF should be one. VAF will be one when GSC is 35 i.e. half of 70. So in order to complete value "1" value "0.65" is taken. Note value is 0.35 when GSC is 35 to complete the one factor "0.65" is required.

But following is the main problem related to GSC. GSC is applied throughout FP even when some GSC does not apply to whole function points. Here's the example to demonstrate GSC problem.

Let's take 11th GSC factor "installation ease". The project is of 100 UAFP and there is no consideration of installation previously by client so the 11th factor is zero.

GSC with installation ease with ZERO	
GSC	**Value(0-5)**
Data communications	1
Distributed data processing	1
Performance	4
Heavily used configuration	0
Transaction rate	1
On-Line data entry	0
End-user efficiency	4
On-Line update	0
Complex processing	0
Reusability	3
Installation ease	0
Operational ease	4
Multiple sites	0
Facilitate change	0
Total	**18**

Table: GSC with installation ease zero

VAF = 0.65 + (18/100) = 0.83. So the FP = 100 * 0.83 = 83 Function Points. But later the client demanded for full blown installation for the project with auto updating when new version is released. So we change out GSC table with installation ease to 5.

GSC with installation ease with FIVE	
GSC	**Value(0-5)**
Data communications	1
Distributed data processing	1
Performance	4
Heavily used configuration	0
Transaction rate	1
On-Line data entry	0
End-user efficiency	4
On-Line update	0
Complex processing	0
Reusability	3
Installation ease	5
Operational ease	4
Multiple sites	0
Facilitate change	0
Total 23	

Table: GSC with Installation ease 5

So VAF = 0.65 + (23/100) = 0.88 so the FP = 100 * 0.88 = 88. The difference is of only 5 FP which from no way a proper effort estimate. To make an auto updation for a software versioning can no way be done in 5 function points, just think downloading new version, deleting the old version, updating any database structure changes etc etc. So that's the reason GSC is not accepted in software industry. Best ways is baseline you're UAFP and make your estimation on base of UAFP.

Enhancement Function Points

Major software project fail not because of programmer's or project managers but due to moody and changing customers. In one of our huge projects we had good programmers, very enthusiastic. The project started of well but customer called ten times in a day to change something or other. Believe me programmers get pissed if the customer is changing his plans every fortnight. Well from this book point of view we have to evaluate this changes which can be addition or deletion of requirements. Function point group has come out with a methodology called as "Enhancement Function Points".

Down is the formulae

*Formulae of EFP (Enhanced Function Points) = (ADD + CHGA) * VAFA + (DELFP) * VAFB*

ADD: This is new function points added. This value is achieved by counting all new EP (Elementary process) given in change request.

CHGA: Function points which are affected due to CR. This value is achieved by counting all DET, FTR, ILF, EI, EO and EQ which are affected. Do not count elements which are not affected.

VAFA: This is VAF factor which is because of CR. Example previously the application was desktop and now is changed to web so the GSC factor is affected.

DELFP: When CR is for removing some functionality this value is counted. It's rare that customer removes functionalities (at least in India), but if they ever estimator has to take note of it by counting the deleted elementary process.

VAFB: Again removal affects Value added factor.

Once we are through with calculating enhanced function points, it time to count total function points of the application.

$$Total\ Function\ points = [UFPB + ADD + CHGA] - [CHGB - DELFP]$$

UFPB: Function points previously counted before enhancement.

ADD: Newly added functionality which leads to new function points after enhancements.

CHGA: Changed function points counted after enhancements.

CHGB: Changed function points before enhancements.

DELFP: Deleted function points.

(I)   Can you explain the concept of Use Case's?

Use case is used to capture the functional requirement of a project. Use case describes the functional requirement of a project in terms of actor, roles and sequence of steps.

(I)   Can you explain the concept of Use case points?

Use Case Point is software sizing and measurement based on Use Case Document. "Use Case Point" is based on work by Gustav Karner in 1993. It was written as a diploma thesis at the University of Linkoping. This work is a modification of work by Allen Albrecht on function points.

(B)   What is a use case transaction?

Use case transactions are atomic set of activities which are either performed or not performed at all. For instance below figure 'Atomic' shows the meaning of atomic in context of use case transaction. The first transaction cycle does not show a complete atomic activity; rather the transaction is in between and is not in persistent state. If you see the second transaction cycle it's atomic because after the user sends the email it's in persistent state and is sitting on the mail server.

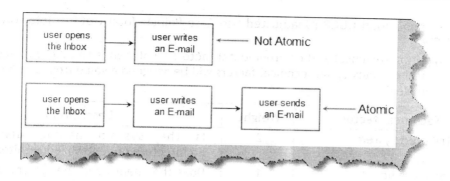

Figure: Atomic

(B) How do we estimate using Use Case Points?

Steps for UCP (Use Case Points) Estimation

· Determine the UAW (Unadjusted Actor weight): The first step is to classify all the actors in to the following classification. Table 'Actor Classification' will give you a clear idea of how to classify the actors. Second column is the litmus test for making a decision of which type of actor falls in which category. The last column provides the factor of complexity.

Classification	Litmus test to recognize classifications	Value/Factor
Simple actors	Simple actors are those which communicate to system through API.	1
Average actors	Average actors are recognized if they have the following properties:	
	· Actors who are interacting with the system through some protocol (HTTP, FTP, or probably some user defined protocol).	
	· Actors which are data stores (Files, RDBMS).	2
Complex	Complex actor is interacting normally through GUI.	3

Table: Actor classification

· Determine number of UUCW (Unadjusted Use case Weight): The second step is to count Use Cases and assign weights depending on number of scenarios and number of transactions.

Use Case Type	Litmus test to decide the Classification	Value/Factor
Simple	Greater than or equal to 3 transactions	5
Average	Between 4 to 7 transactions	10
Complex	Greater than 7 transactions	15

Table: Use case value factor

- Determine Total UUCP (Unadjusted Use Case Point): Total UUCP = Total UAW + Total UUCW.
- Computing technical and environmental factor: Final step is to take into account the technical complexity. All technical factors will be assigned a value from 0 to 5 depending on complexity.

	Technical factor	Weight	Description
t1	Distributed System	2	Is the system having distributed architecture or centralized architecture?
t2	Response time	1	Does the client need the system to fast? Is time response one of the important criteria?
t3	End user efficiency	1	How's the end user's efficiency?
t4	Complex internal processing	1	Is the business process very complex? Like complicated accounts closing, inventory tracking, heavy tax calculation etc.
t5	Reusable code	1	Do we intend to keep the reusability high? So will increase the design complexity.
t6	Installation ease	0.5	Is client looking for installation ease? By default, we get many installers which create packages. But the client might be looking for some custom installation, probably depending on modules. One of our client has a requirement that when the client wants to install, he can choose which modules he can install. Is the requirement such that when there is a new version there should be auto installation? These factors will count when assigning value to this factor.
t7	Easy use	0.5	Is user friendliness a top priority?
t8	Portable	2	Is the customer also looking for cross platform implementation?
t9	Easy to change	1	Is the customer looking for high customization in the future? That also increases the architecture design complexity and hence this factor.
t10	Concurrent	1	Is the customer looking at large number of users working with locking support? This will increase the architecture complexity and hence this value.
t11	Security objectives	1	Is the customer looking at having heavy security like SSL? Or do we have to write custom code logic for encryption?

| t12 | Direct access to third parties | 1 | Does the project depend in using third party controls? For understanding the third-party controls and studying its pros and cons, considerable effort will be required. So, this factor should be rated accordingly. |
| t13 | User training facilities | 1 | Will the software from user perspective be so complex that separate training has to be provided? So this factor will vary accordingly. |

Table: Technical Factor

- Equation for Tfactor = sum(T1....T13)
- TCF (Technical Complexity Factor): TCF = 0.6 + (0.01 * Tfactor).
- EF (Environmental Factor): There are other factors like trained staff, motivation of programmers etc. which have quiet a decent impact on the cost estimate.

	Environmental Factor	Weight	Description
e1	Familiarity with project	1.5	1.5Are all the people working in the project familiar with domain and technical details of the project? Probably you will spend most of your time in explaining them all know-how's.
e2	Application experience	0.5	How much is the application experience?
e3	Object-oriented programming experience	1	As use-case documents are inputs to object oriented design, it's important that people on the project should have basic knowledge of OOP concepts.
e4	Lead analyst capability	0.5	How is the analyst who is leading the project? Does he have enough knowledge of the domain?.
e5	Motivation	1	Are the programmers motivated for working on the project? Instability in the project will always lead to people leaving half way through their source code. And the hand over becomes really tough. This factor you can put according to how software industry is going on? Example, if the software market is very good, put this at maximum value. More good the market, more the jobs and more the programmers will jump.
e6	Stable requirements	2	Is the client clear of what he wants? I have seen clients' expectations are the most important factor in the stability of requirements. If the client is of highly

			changing nature, put this value to maximum.
e7	Part-time Staff	-1	Are there part-time staff in projects, like consultants etc.?
e8	Difficult programming language	-1	How much is the language complexity, Assembly, VB 6.0, C++, C etc.

Table: Environmental factor

- Efactor = SUM(e1...e8).
- Calculating Environmental Factor = EF = 1.4 + (-0.03 * Efactor).
- AUCP (Adjusted Use Case Points). Finally, calculating the Adjusted Use case points: AUCP = UUCP * TCF * EF
- Multiplying by Man/Hours Factor: AUCP * Person/Hours/AUCP.

Karner[13] proposed a factor of 20 staff hours per Use Case point for a project estimate. While Sharks states that field experience has shown that effort can range from 15 to 30 hours per Use Case point.Schneider and Winters proposed number of staff hours per Use Case point depends on the environmental factors. The number of factors in E1 through E6 that are below 3 are counted and added to the number of factors in E7 through E8 that are above 3. If the total is 2 or less, the general idea is to use twenty staff hours per UCP; if the total is 3 or 4, use twenty-eight staff hours per UCP. If the number exceeds 5, it is usually recommended that changes should be made to the project so the number can be adjusted, because in this case, the risk is unacceptably high. Another possibility is to increase the number of staff hours to thirty-six per

Sample project scope (Sample Data Entry Project):

Let's start with a sample fiction project. Here's the scope of the project. TNC company till now·was using manual way of maintaining its customer database and there credit card information. Data entry operator manually validates credit card information from external payment gateway. They maintain customer code, customer name, customer address, customer phone and validated customer credit card information in Customer registry. Customer code is unique for a customer. So, TNC manually checks for the validations and enters in the customer registry. TNC wants the data entry project to be automated. TNC is looking for the following automation:

- Customer code assigned should be checked for uniqueness automatically.
- Customer code should not exceed 8 length.
- Credit card validation should be automatic for the current system. TNC has already given the API documentation of how to interact with the third party payment system.
- Credit card length should not exceed more than 10 length.
- Data entry operator should be able to add/update/delete customer information.
- The database will be in the TNC head office and only data entry operators will be allowed to use the data entry software.
- Software should work on Windows platform. At this moment, TNC has Windows 2000 client installed in all computers.

Writing Use Case for Sample Data Entry Project:

I have used Alistair Cockburn's template for the "Use Case point" example. Use Case template varies from person to person, project to project, and organization to organization. I found Alistair's template to be complete, so just took it. But there's no hard and fast rule that you have to follow this template. What will matter is what steps you write in the Use Case.

Use Case Transactions: It's an atomic set of activities that are either performed entirely or not all. What is a Use Case transaction and what's not: just see if the transaction is adding any business value or else do not include it as a transaction. Example: the user switches on the computer, user clicks on add button or any GUI, are not valid business transaction steps. But the customer code validated for credit card information is a valid business transaction. Use Case points are heavily affected by the way the Actors and their transactions are identified. So a Use Case Document should be written by predefined guidelines, uniformly in a project. Just take a meeting with the whole project team before starting writing Use Cases. The depth of the Use Case Document will affect estimation by 40%.

Use Case #	DATAENTRYPROJECTCUST-1009
Use Case name	Maintain Customer
Description	This Use Case depicts full maintenance of customer from project "Data Entry".
Scope and level	Data Entry System (Internal) Credit Card System (External)
Level	User Goal Level (If this property is not understood, look at the reference for the book Writing Effective Use Cases (**PRE-PUB. DRAFT#3**): Alistair Cockburn Humans and technology)
Primary and secondary actors	Data Entry operator.
Stakeholders and interests	
Trigger	Data entry operator clicks on menu: "Add New Customer"
Preconditions	Data entry operator should be logged in. Data entry operator should have access to Internet.
Assumptions	Customer information received is entered manually. No automated import routine is in the scope.
Failed End condition	Customer is not added to database and appropriate error message is displayed. Customer code already existing in the customer database. Customer code length limit is exceeded. Customer credit card limit is exceeded. Customer credit card validation failed with the payment gateway.
Action	Add new customer
Main success scenario (or basic Flow):	Data entry operator receives customer information. Data entry operator enters following information: Customer code Customer name Customer address Customer phone Customer code is checked if it exists in Customer table. If the

	customer code is existing then "Duplicate Customer Code" error is raised. If the customer code is more than 8 length, then "Customer code length limit crossed" error is raised. After step 3 is passed OK. Data entry operator enters credit card information. If the credit card length is more than 10 length, then "Credit card length limit crossed" error is raised. Credit card information is send to the external payment gateway. Appropriate APIs of the external payment gateway will be used for validity. External payment gateway returns "OK" if credit card is validated or else will return "NOT VALID" flag. Data entry operator then adds the customer in database.
Alternate scenario (Extensions):	Update Existing Customer Data entry operator enters customer code to retrieve the customer who has to be updated. Data entry operator makes appropriate changes to the customer information. All steps and business validation from 1 to 6 of Add new Customer is repeated. Data Entry operator updates the customer information.
Alternate scenario (Extensions):	Delete Existing Customer Data entry operator enters customer code to retrieve the customer who has to be deleted. Data entry operator deletes the customer. Data entry operator is alerted "Are you sure you want to delete the Customer?" If the data entry operator clicks "Yes", then the customer is deleted from the database. If the data entry operator clicks "NO", no action is taken.
Success Guarantee (Post conditions):	Customer is added to Customer database. Customer is updated to Customer database. Customer is deleted from Customer database.
Special Requirements (including business rules):	
Technology and Data Variations List:	If credit card payment gateway API changes, the interaction of the data entry customer module will have to be changed accordingly.
Frequency of occurrence:	
Notes and Open Issues:	

Table 6.0

Applying Use Case Points:

Let's start applying Use Case Points to the above given document.

- Determining Unadjusted Use Actor Weights (UAW): In this project, we have identified only one actor "Data Entry Operator". The upper Actor (data entry operator) is complex as data entry operator will be interacting through GUI. So UAW=3 as per Table:2.0.
- Determine number of UUCW (Unadjusted Use case Weight): There are 12 transactions

[Adding also the alternative flows] in Table 6.0 Use Case. So the above Use Case is complex according to Table 'Use case value factor'. So referring Table 'Use case value factor', UUCW=15.

· Now calculating the total UUCP = 15 + 3 = 18.

· Determining the technical factor

	Technical factor	Weight	Value	Weighted Value	Explanation
t1	Distributed System	2	1	2	Simple two tier architecture is decided.
t2	Response time	1	4	4	Speed is of importance as the data entry operator has to enter data quiet fast.
t3	End user efficiency	1	3	3	Data entry operator has high user efficiency.
t4	Complex Internal Processing	1	2	2	Its simple entry screen and no business process has been scoped by the client. Only credit card check and duplicate customer code is the business check.
t5	Reusable Code	1	1	1	No reusability as project is small and customer is not looking for any further changes for at least two years.
t6	Installation Ease	0.5	0	0	TNC has good in house development team, and installation problems will be handled by them. Technology thought is C#, and .NET setup wizard will be enough to make the installation process easy.
t7	Easy use	0.5	4	2	Yes, data entry operator has to have user friendly menus and shortcut keys for fast entry of data.
t8	Portable	2	1	2	TNC has Windows 2000 client as specified in the scope document.
t9	Easy to change	1	0	0	None specified by client.
t10	Concurrent	1	0	0	Client has not clarified about this issue as such in the scope document. So assumed least concurrent.
t11	Security objectives	1	0	0	None specified by client. Even credit card information will be passed with

					out encryption.
t12	Direct access to third parties	1	3	3	Using the credit card check API.
t13	User training facilities	1	0	0	The screen is simple, and data entry operator can operate without any training.
	Total			19	

Table 7.0

· Depending on the table, calculating the Technical Factor: TCF = 0.6 + (0.01 * Tfactor) = 0.6 + (0.01 * 19) = 0.79
· Calculating environmental factor

	Environmental Factor	Value	Weight	Weighted Columns	Explanation for the value assigned
e1	Familiarity with project	5	1.5	7.5	It's a simple project, so familiarity with project is not so much needed.
e2	Application experience	5	0.5	2.5	It's a simple application.
e3	Object-oriented programming experience	5	1	5	Every one has good OOP knowledge.
e4	Lead analyst capability	5	0.5	2.5	It's a simple project; no lead analyst needed till now.
e5	Motivation	1	1	1	Motivation is little down as programmers are reluctant to work on the project because of its simplicity.
e6	Stable requirements	4	2	8	Client is very clear with what he wants?
e7	Part-time Staff	0	-1	0	No part time staff.
e8	Difficult programming language.	3	-1	-3	C# will be used. And most of the programming guys are new to C# and .NET technology.

Table 8.0

According to [Kirsten Ribu Master of Science Thesis], Environmental factor plays a very important role in the estimation. A slight variation will increase the Use Case point by a very, very drastic amount. Even small adjustments of an environmental factor, for instance by half a point, can make a great difference to the estimate. Difference of 3 to 2.5 increased the estimate by 4580 hours, from 10831 to 15411 hours, or 42.3 percent. This means that if the values for the environmental factors are not set correctly, there may be disastrous .

- Using formulae for calculating EF = 1.4 + (-0.03 * Efactor) = 1.4 + (-0.03 * 23.5) = 0.695.
- Calculating AUCP = UUCP * TCF * EF = 18 X 0.79 X 0.695 = 9.88 approx = 10 Use Case Points. I have done the approximation as its only creates 3 to 4 hours of difference.
- Calculating according to Karner, i.e., 20 staff hours per Use Case points = 10 X 20 = 200 hours for the total project. If programmer works for 8 hours for a day, then 340/8 = 25 days.
- Calculating according to Schneider and Winters, from e1 to e6 there are only 3 properties that are below 3. And from e7 to e8, there are none whose value is above 3. So the total is 3. We use 28 staff hours. 10 X 28 = 280 hours.

If programmer works for 8 hours, then 35 days. If this step is not understood, look at the steps defined in theory of Use Case points. If we apply sixth sense, we will find Karner approach is coming to round about figure. It really depends what you want to follow: Karner or Schneider approach. Best is that after two or three projects, whatever is coming accurate from history, take that approach. Best approach is to use Excel and incorporate formulas properly.

> **Note:** *Check for the use case points estimation sheet in the CD.*

(A) Can you explain on what basis does TPA actually work?

> **Note:** *TPA analysis is used to estimate black box testing. If you are project manager of a project which is a pure testing project TPA can comes as a help to you.*

There are three main elements which determine estimate for black box test Size, Test strategy and Productivity. Using all these three elements we can determine the estimate for black box testing for a given project. So let's understand all these elements step by step.

Size: The prime important thing in estimation is definitely the size of the project. Size of a project is mainly defined by number of function points. But a function point fails or pays least importance to the following factors:

- Complexity: Complexity means how many conditions exist in function points identified during project. If more conditions means more test cases that means more testing estimates. For instance below is an application which takes customer name from the end user. If the customer name is greater than 20 characters then application should throw an error. So for this case there will be one test case. But let's say the end user also puts one more condition that if the user inputs any invalid character then the application should throw an error. Because there is one more extra condition in the project that means the complexity has increased due to the extra condition which also means that we need now two test cases to test, which means increase in test efforts. Below figure signifies the same in a pictorial manner.

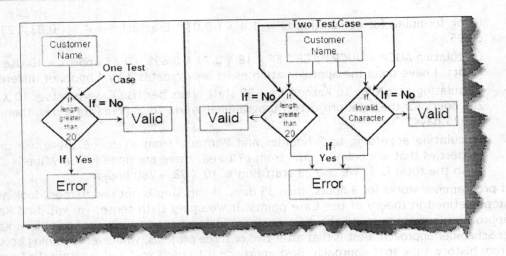

Figure: Complexity

- **Interfacing:**How much does one function affect the other part of the system?. So if this function is modified then accordingly the other systems have to be tested as this function has high impact analysis.
- **Uniformity**: How reusable is the application?. It is important to consider how many similar structured functions exist in the system. It is important to consider the extent to which the system allows testing with slight modifications.

Test strategy: Every project has certain requirements. The importance of all these requirements also affects testing estimates. Any requirement importance is from two perspectives one is the user importance and one the user usage. Depending on these two characteristics a requirement rating can be generated and a strategy can be chalked out accordingly. Which also means that estimates vary accordingly?.

Productivity: This is one more important aspect to be considered while estimating black box testing. Productivity depends on lot of aspects for instance if your project has fresher's definitely your estimates shoot up, because you will need to train the fresher's in terms of project and domain knowledge. Productivity has two important aspects environment and productivity figure. Environmental factor defines how much the environment affects a project estimate. Environmental factors contains aspects like tools, test environments, availability if test ware etc. While productivity figure depends on knowledge, how many senior people are there in the team etc?

Below diagram shows the complete pictorial regarding the different elements which constitute TPA analysis as discussed in the previous section.

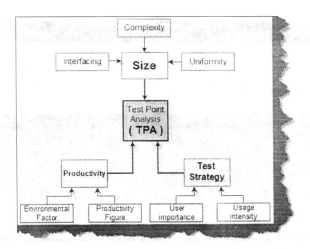

Figure: TPA parameters

(A) How did you do estimation for black box testing?

> ***Note:*** *In CD we have provided "FunctionPoints (Accounting Application).xls",*
> *which is used in this example to make TPA calculation easier.*

In order to really answer this question let's do one complete estimation practically for a sample project. Below is a simple accounting application developed for http:// www.questpond.com (that's my official website) website to track its sales. The first screen is a voucher entry screen. It's a normal simple voucher entry screen with an extra functionality to print the voucher. The second screen is a master screen to add accounting codes.

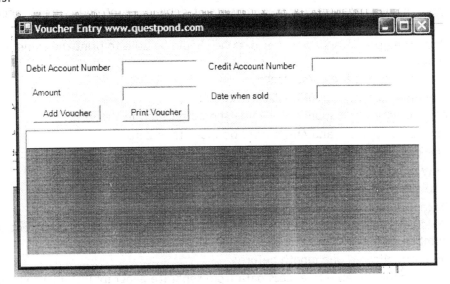

Figure: Accounting application

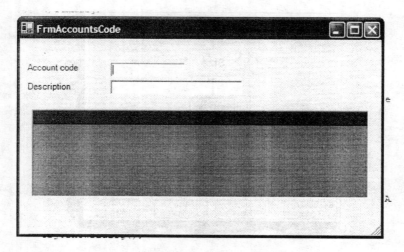

Figure: Account code description

Below are point wise requirements gathered from the end customer:

1. The account code entered in the voucher entry screen should be a valid account code from the defined chart of accounts by the customer.

2. User should be able to add, delete and modify account code from the chart of account master (This is what exactly the second screen defines).

3. User will not be able to delete chart of account code if he has already entered transactions for the same in vouchers.

4. Chart of account code master will consist of account code and description of the account code.

5. Account code can not be greater than 10.

6. The voucher data entry screen consists of debit account code, credit account code, date of transaction and amount.

7. Once the user enters a voucher data he should be able to print the same in future any time.

8. The dr & cr a/c are compulsory

9. The Amount value should not be negative

10. After pressing the submit the value should be seen in the grid

11. Amt is compulsory and Amt should be more than zero.

12. The debit and credit account should be equal in value.

13. Only numeric and non-negative values are allowed in amount field.

14. Two types of entry are allowed i.e.sales and commission.

15. Date, amount and voucher number is compulsory.

16. Voucher number should be in serial wise and system should auto increment the voucher number with every voucher added.

17. No entry allowed one month before.

18. Users should be able to access data from separate geographical location. For instance

if one user is working in India and the other in China, then both user should be able to access each others data through their respective location.

Now that we have all the requirements lets try to estimate how we can use TPA to do get the actual man days. Below figure shows our road map how we will achieve the same using TPA. There are in all ten steps to achieve the same.

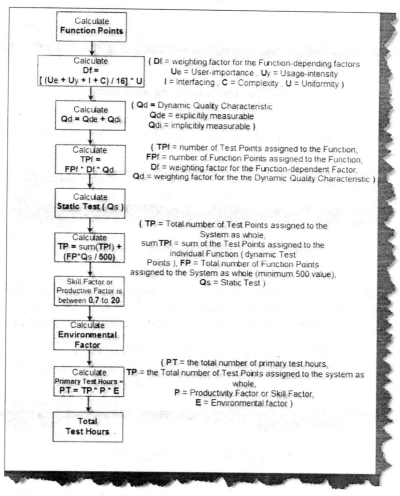

Figure: TPA steps.

Step 1: Calculate function points

> **Note:** *You will not able to follow this if you have not read the function points explanation previously.*

EI calculation

Below are the EI entries for the accounting application. Currently we have two screens one is the master screen and one is the voucher transaction screen. In the description we have also described which DET's we have considered. For the add voucher screen we have 7 DET (note the buttons are also counted as DET) and for the Account code master we have 4 DET.

Functionality	DET	FTR	Value	Description
Add voucher	7	1	3	DET :- Debit account code , Credit Account code , Amount , Date , Add voucher button , Print voucher button and display grid
Add account code	4	1	3	DET:- Account code , Add button , unselect all button and Grid

Figure: EI for the accounting application

EIF

There are no EIF's in the system because we do not communicate with any external application.

Functionality	DET	RET	Value	Description
NA	NA	NA	NA	NA

Figure: EIF for the accounting application

EO

EO's are nothing but complex report. In our system we have three complex reports Trial balance, Profit and loss and Balance sheet. By default we have assumed 20 fields which makes it a complex report (When we do estimation some times assumptions are fine).

Functionality	DET	FTR	Value	Description
Report Trial Balance	20	1	5	Assumed maximum 20 fields
Profit and Loss	20	1	5	Assumed maximum 20 fields
Balance sheet	20	1	5	Assumed maximum 20 fields

Figure: EO for the accounting application

EQ

EQ's are nothing but simple output sent from the inside of the application to the external world. For instance simple report is typical type of EQ's. In our current accounting application we have one simple print that is the print voucher. We have assumed 20 DET's for the same so that we can move ahead with the calculation.

Functionality	DET	FTR	Value	Description
Print voucher	20	1	4	Assumed 20 DET's

Figure: EQ for the accounting application

GSC calculation

As said in the FPA tutorial previously GSC factor defines the other factor of the projects which the FP counting does not accommodate. For the accounting application we have kept all the GSC factors are 1 except for two GSC factor Data communications and performance. We have kept communication as 2 because one the requirement point is that we need application data to be accessed from multiple centers which increases the data communication complexity. Other GSC factor we have considered a bit complex is the performance because one of the requirement of the end customer is that performance should be averagely good. Below figure shows the GSC entries.

GSC Attribute	Definitions	Value
Data communications:	How many communication facilities are there to aid in the transfer or exchange of information with the application or system?	2
Distributed data processing	How are distributed data and processing functions handled?	0
Performance	Did the user require response time or throughput?	2
Heavily used configuration	How heavily used is the current hardware platform where the application will be executed?	1
Transaction rate	How frequently are transactions executed; daily, weekly, monthly, etc.?	1
On-Line data entry	What percentage of the information is entered On-Line?	1
End-user efficiency	Was the application designed for end-user efficiency?	1
On-Line update	How many ILF's are updated by On-Line transaction?	1
Complex processing	Does the application have extensive logical or mathematical processing?	1
Reusability	Was the application developed to meet one or many user's needs?	1
Installation ease	How difficult is conversion and installation?	1
Operational ease	How effective and/or automated are start-up, back up, and recovery procedures?	1
Multiple sites	Was the application specifically designed, developed, and supported to be installed at multiple sites for multiple organizations?	1
Facilitate change	Was the application specifically designed, developed, and supported to facilitate change?	1
GSC		0.8

Figure: GSC factors for accounting application

Total calculation

Now that we have filled in all the details we need to calculate the total man days. Below is the image which will explain us how the calculations are done. The first five rows i.e. ILF, EIF, EO, EQ and EI are nothing but total of the individual entries. A total unadjusted function point is the total of ILF + EIF + EO + EQ + EI. We get the total adjusted function which is nothing but Total Un-Adjusted function points multiplied by the GSC factor. Depending on organization base line we define how much FP can be completed by a programmer in one day. For instance for the below accounting application we have put 1.2 FP per day. Depending on the FP per day we get total man days. Once we have got total man days we distribute these values across the phases. One of the very important thing what we have just got is the total execution time. So we have assigned the total man days to the execution phase. From the execution phase man days we distribute 20 percent to requirement phase, 20 percent to technical design and 5 percent to testing.

> **Note:** *We will answer a small and sweet answer in this mid of the explanation.*

(A) How did you estimate white box testing?

The testing estimates derived from function points is actually the estimates for only white box testing. So in the below figure 1.3 man days is actually the estimate for white box testing of the project. It does not take in to account black box testing estimation.

(A) Is there a way to estimate acceptance test cases in a system?

Total acceptance test cases = total adjusted function points multiplied by 1.2

The total estimate for this project is 37.7 man days.

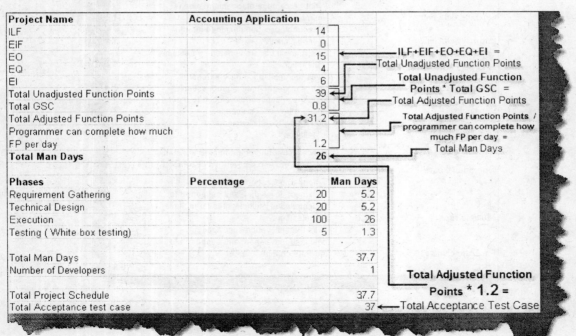

Figure: Total estimation of the accounting application

Now that we have completed the function point analysis for this project lets move to the second step to calculate black box testing using TPA.

Step 2: Calculate Df (Function dependant factors)

Df is defined for each function point. So all the function point description as well as value is taken and Df is calculated for each of them. You can see from the figure below how every function point factor is take and Df calculated for the same.

function\factors	TPf	FPf	Ue	Uy	I	C	U	Df
					$Df = ((Ue + Uy + I + C) / 16)$ * U			
Voucher data	14.84	7	12	12	2	3	1	1.81
chart of accounts data	5.12	7	3	2	2	3	1	0.63
Report trail balance	4.75	5	3	2	2	6	1	0.81
Report profit and loss	4.75	5	3	2	2	6	1	0.81
Report balance sheet	4.75	5	3	2	2	6	1	0.81
Print voucher	9.36	4	12	12	2	6	1	2.00
add Voucher	8.34	3	12	12	2	12	1	2.38
Add account code	3.29	3	6	2	4	3	1	0.94

Figure: Df calculated

But we have still not seen how Df will be calculated. Df is calculated using four inputs User importance, Usage intensity, Interfacing and Complexity. Below figure show the different inputs in a pictorial manner. All the four factors are rated with Low, Normal and High and assigned to each function factors derived from function points. So let's understand these factors step by step.

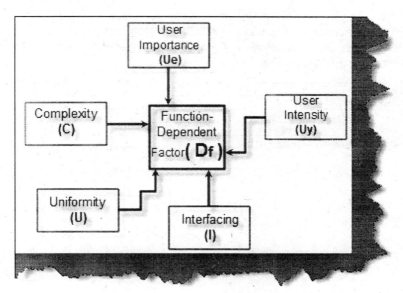

Figure: Factors on which Df depends

User importance (Ue): How important is this function factor to the user and compared to other function factors. Below figure shows how they are rated. Voucher data, Print voucher and Add voucher is rated with high user importance. With out these the user can not work at all. Reports have been rated low because they do not really stop the user from working, definitely they are of high importance but not as high as the add voucher and print voucher. Chart of accounts master is rated low because the master data is something which is added one time and can also be added from the back end.

User importance (Ue)		
Rating		**Description**
3	Low	The importance of the function relative to the other function is low.
6	Normal	The importance of the function relative to the other function is normal.
12	High	The importance of the function relative to the other function is high.

function\factors	TPf	FPf	Ue	Uy	I	C	U	Df
Voucher data	14.84	7	12	12	2	3	1	1.81
chart of accounts data	5.12	7	3	2	2	3	1	0.63
Report trail balance	4.75	5	3	2	2	6	1	0.81
Report profit and loss	4.75	5	3	2	2	6	1	0.81
Report balance sheet	4.75	5	3	2	2	6	1	0.81
Print voucher	9.36	4	12	12	2	6	1	2.00
add Voucher	8.34	3	12	12	2	12	1	2.38
Add account code	3.29	3	6	2	4	3	1	0.94

Figure: User importance

Usage intensity (Uy): This factor tells how many users use it and how often. Below figure shows how we have assigned the values to each function factors. Add voucher, print voucher and voucher data is the most used function factors, hence they are rated high. Other all function factors are rated as low.

Usage intensity (Uy)		
Rating		**Description**
2	Low	The function is only used a few times per day or per week.
4	Normal	The function is being used a great many times per day.
12	High	The function is used continuously throughout the day.

function\factors	TPf	FPf	Ue	Uy	I	C	U	Df
Voucher data	14.84	7	12	12	2	3	1	1.81
chart of accounts data	5.12	7	3	2	2	3	1	0.63
Report trail balance	4.75	5	3	2	2	6	1	0.81
Report profit and loss	4.75	5	3	2	2	6	1	0.81
Report balance sheet	4.75	5	3	2	2	6	1	0.81
Print voucher	9.36	4	12	12	2	6	1	2.00
add Voucher	8.34	3	12	12	2	12	1	2.38
Add account code	3.29	3	6	2	4	3	1	0.94

Figure: Usage intensity

Interfacing (I): This factor defines how much impact does this function factor affect the other parts of the system. But how do we now find the impact?. In TPA concept of LDS affected is used to determine the interfacing rating. LDS means logical data source. In our project we have two logical data source one is Voucher data and the other is the Account code data (i.e. Chart of accounts data). Following are the important points to be noted which determine the interfacing:

· We need to consider only functions which modify LDS. If a function is not modifying LDS then its rating is LOW by default.

· To define LDS we need to define how many LDS is affected by the function and how many other functions access the LDS. Other functions only need to access the function, even if they do not modify its still considered.

Below is the table which defines complexity level according to number of LDS and Functions impacting on the LDS.

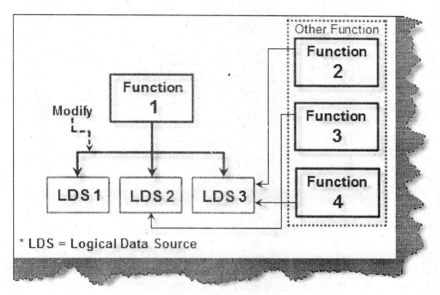

Figure: LDS and the function concept

LDS ↓	Functions →		
	1	2 to 5	greater than 5
1	L	L	A
2 to 5	L	A	H
greater than 5	A	H	H
(* L = Low, A = Average, H = High)			

Figure: LDS ratings

So now depending on the two points defined above lets try to find out the interfacing value for our accounting project. As said previously we have two functions which modify LDS in our project one is the Add Voucher which affects the Voucher data and Add account code which affects the Chart of Accounts code (i.e. the Accounts code master). So first let's see Add voucher function, below is the diagram which explains in detail which LDS and functions are involved in the same. Add voucher primarily affects Voucher data LDF. But other functions like reports and print also use the LDS. So in total there are five numbers of functions and one LDS. Now looking at the number of LDS and number of function table the impact complexity factor is LOW.

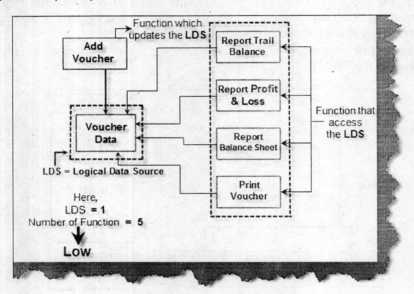

Figure: Add voucher data

The other function which does modification is the Add account code. The LDS affected is the chart of account code and the function which affects it is the Add account code function. There are other functions who indirectly affect this function for instance report which needs to access account code, print voucher which uses the account code to print account description and also the Add voucher function uses the chart of accounts code LDS to validate if the account code is proper or not. So again we see the look up table and the impact complexity factor is AVERAGE.

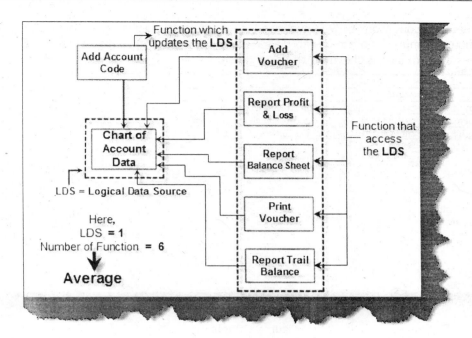

Figure: Add account code LDS and functions

The other function factors do not modify any data so we give them a LOW rating. Below is the interfacing complexity factor assigned below.

Interfacing (I)		
Rating		**Description**
2	Low	The degree of interfacing associated with the function is low.
4	Normal	The degree of interfacing associated with the function is normal.
8	High	The degree of interfacing associated with the function is high.

function\factors	TPf	FPf	Ue	Uy	I	C	U	Df
Voucher data	14.84	7	12	12	2	3	1	1.81
chart of accounts data	5.12	7	3	2	2	3	1	0.63
Report trail balance	4.75	5	3	2	2	6	1	0.81
Report profit and loss	4.75	5	3	2	2	6	1	0.81
Report balance sheet	4.75	5	3	2	2	6	1	0.81
Print voucher	9.36	4	12	12	2	6	1	2.00
add Voucher	8.34	3	12	12	2	12	1	2.38
Add account code	3.29	3	6	2	4	3	1	0.94

Figure: Interfacing

Complexity (C): This factor defines how complex is the algorithm for the particular function factor. Add voucher is the most complex functionality in the project and it can have more than eleven conditions so we have rated the Complexity factor as the highest. Reports are mediumly complex and can be rated as averagely complex. So as discussed we have assigned values accordingly as shown in the figure below.

Complexity (C)		
Rating		**Description**
3	Low	The function contains no more than five conditions.
6	Normal	The function contains between six and eleven conditions.
12	High	The function contains more than eleven conditions.

function\factors	TPf	FPf	Ue	Uy	I	C	U	Df
Voucher data	14.84	7	12	12	2	3	1	1.81
chart of accounts data	5.12	7	3	2	2	3	1	0.63
Report trail balance	4.75	5	3	2	2	6	1	0.81
Report profit and loss	4.75	5	3	2	2	6	1	0.81
Report balance sheet	4.75	5	3	2	2	6	1	0.81
Print voucher	9.36	4	12	12	2	6	1	2.00
add Voucher	8.34	3	12	12	2	12	1	2.38
Add account code	3.29	3	6	2	4	3	1	0.94

Figure: Complexity

Uniformity (U): This factor defines how reusable is the system. For instance if a test case written for one function can be again applied then it affects the testing estimates accordingly. Currently for this project we have taken a uniformity factor of 1. So for example if the customer had a requirement to also update accounts code. Then we could have had two functions i.e. Add voucher and update voucher, but the test case for both of them are same only with minimal change.

Uniformity . (U)	
Rating	**Description**
0.6	In the case of a second occurrence of a virtually unique function :in such cases, the test specifications can be largely reused
0.6	In the case of a clone function: the test specifications can be reused for clone functions.
0.6	In the case of a dummy function (provided that reusable test specifications have already been drawn up for the dummy).
1	Otherwise Uniformity factor is 1

function\factors	TPf	FPf	Ue	Uy	I	C	U	Df
Voucher data	14.84	7	12	12	2	3	1	1.81
chart of accounts data	5.12	7	3	2	2	3	1	0.63
Report trail balance	4.75	5	3	2	2	6	1	0.81
Report profit and loss	4.75	5	3	2	2	6	1	0.81
Report balance sheet	4.75	5	3	2	2	6	1	0.81
Print voucher	9.36	4	12	12	2	6	1	2.00
add Voucher	8.34	3	12	12	2	12	1	2.38
Add account code	3.29	3	6	2	4	3	1	0.94

Figure: Uniformity

One we have all the five factors we apply the below formulae to calculate Df for all the function factors.

$$Df = [(Ue + Uy + I + C) / 16] * U$$

Step 3: Calculate Qd:

The third step is to calculate Qd. Qd i.e dynamic quality characteristics has two parts one is the explicit characteristic (Qde) and other is implicit (Qdi). Qde has five important characteristics Functionality, Security, Suitability, Performance and Portability. Below diagram shows how we rate those ratings. Qdi define the implicit characteristic part of the Qd. These are not standard and vary from project to project. For instance we have identified for this accounting application four characteristics user friendly, efficiency, performance and maintainability. From these four characteristics which ever are important we assign 0.02 value for the same. We can see from the below figure for user friendliness we have assigned 0.02 value other are left. In Qde part we have given functionality normal importance and performance as relatively unimportant but we do need to account the same. Once we have Qde and Qdi then Qd = Qde + Qdi. For this sample you can see that the total value of Qd is 1.17 (which is obtained from 1.15 + 0.02).

Qd is calculated using the rating multiplied by the value. The below table shows the rating and the next after it shows the actual value. So the 1.15 has come from the below formulae

$$((5 * 0.75) + (3 * 0.05) + (4 * 0.10) + (3 * 0.10) + (3 * .10)) / 4$$

Characteristics\Rating	0	3	4	5	6
functionality	(Weighting 0.75)				
security	(Weighting 0.05)				
Usability	(Weighting 0.10)				
Efficiency	(Weighting 0.10)				

Figure: Qd ratings

1) Dynamic quality characteristics (Qd)		Dynamic quality characteristics (Qd)	
((0,3,4,5,6)*we		**Rating**	**Description**
functionality	5		
security	3	0	Quality requirement are not important and are therefore disregarded for test purposes.
suitability	4		
performance	3	3	Quality requirement are relatively unimportant but do need to be taken into consideration for test purposes.
portability	3		
Q de	1.15		
userfriendliness	0.02	4	Quality requirement are of normal importance. (This rating is generally appropriate where the information system relates to a support process.)
efficiency	0		
performance	0	5	Quality requirements are very important. (This rating is generally appropriate where the information system relates to a primary process.)
maintainability	0		
Q di	0.02	6	Quality requirement are extremely important.
Q dynamic	1.17	(Qd=Qde +Qdi)	

Figure: Calculation of Qd (Dynamic characteristic)

Step 4 Calculate TPf for each function:

In this step we calculate TPf (number of test points assigned to each function). This is done by using three data values (FPf, Df and Qd) calculated till now, below is the formulae for the same.

$$TPf = FPf * Df * Qd$$

Because we are using the excel sheet these calculations happen automatically. Below figure which shows how the TPf calculations are done.

functionality	5	(weight factor 0,75)						
security	3	(weight factor 0,05)						
suitability	4	(weight factor 0,10)						
performance	3	(weight factor 0,05)						
portability	3	(weight factor 0,05)						
Q de	**1.15**			explicitly measurable				
userfriendliness	0.02	(weight factor 0,02)						
efficiency	0	(weight factor 0,02)						
performance	0	(weight factor 0,02)						
maintainability	0	(weight factor 0,02)						
Q di	**0.02**			implicitly measurable				
Q dynamic	**1.17**	(Qd=Qde +Qdi)						

2) Function dependent variables (Df) and test points (TPf)

Df=((Ue+Uy+I+C)/16)*U

TPf=FPf*Df*Qd

TPf = FPf * Df * Qd

function\factors	TPf	FPf	Ue	Uy	I	C	U	Df
Voucher data	14.84	7	12	12	2	3	1	1.81
chart of accounts data	5.12	7	3	2	2	3	1	0.63
Report trail balance	4.75	5	3	2	2	6	1	0.81
Report profit and loss	4.75	5	3	2	2	6	1	0.81
Report balance sheet	4.75	5	3	2	2	6	1	0.81
Print voucher	9.36	4	12	12	2	6	1	2.00
add Voucher	8.34	3	12	12	2	12	1	2.38
Add account code	3.29	3	6	2	4	3	1	0.94

Figure: Calculation of TPf

Step 5 Calculate static test points Qs:

In this step we take in to account the static quality characteristic of the project. This is done by defining a check list and then if the test team needs to consider them we assign a value of 16 to those properties. For this project we have only considered easy to use as a criteria and hence assigned 16 to it.

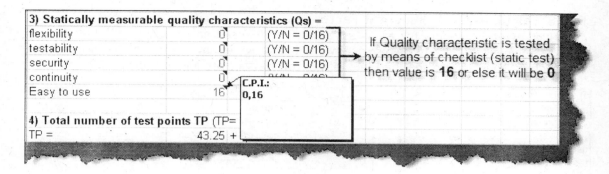

Figure: Qs calculation

Step 6 calculate total number of test points:

Now that we have TPf's for all function factors, FP and Qs (static test point data), its time to calculate Tp (Total number of test points).

$$Tp = sum(TPf) + (FP*Qs / 500)$$

For the accounting system total Tp = 71.21 (use a calculator to check it out yourself, just makes the concept better to understand). Below is the figure which shows how the total Tp is derived.

4) Total number of test points TP (TP= sum(TPf) + (FP*Qs)/500)					
TP =	55.21 + (	500	*	16	) / 500
TOTAL NUMBER OF TEST POINTS			**71.21**		

Step 7 calculate Productivity / Skill factor:

Productivity / Skill factor shows the number of test hours needed per test points. It's a measure of experience, knowledge, and expertise and teams ability to perform. Productivity factor vary from project to project and also organization to organization. For instance if we have project team with many seniors then the productivity increases. But if we have fresher's who are just learning then definitely the productivity decreases. Higher the productivity factor higher is the number of test hours required.

For this project we have considered we have good resources and with great ability. So we have entered a value of 1.50 which means we have considered the highest productivity.

6) Primary test hours (PT=TP*Skill*E)				Skill Factor or Productivity factor
Skill factor	1.50			is considered between **0.7 o 2.0**
PT=	68.14	*	1.50	*	0.95
TOTAL PRIMARY HOURS			**97.34**	

Figure: Productivity factor / Skill factor

Step 8 Calculate environmental Factor (E):

Number of test hours for each test point is influenced not only by skills but also the environment in which those resources work. Below figure shows the different environmental factors. You can also see the table ratings for every environmental factor.

5) Environmental factor E =	
test tools	2
Development testing	8
test basis	3
development environm	2
test environment	1
testware	4

Testware	
Rating	Description
1	A usable general initial data set (tables, etc) and specified test cases are available for the test.
2	A usable general initial data set (tables, etc) is available for the test.
4	No usable testware is available.

Figure: Testware

5) Environmental factor E =	
test tools	2
Development testing	8
test basis	3
development environm	2
test environment	1
testware	4

Test tools	
Rating	Description
1	Testing involves the use of a query language such as SQL: a record and playback tool is also being used.
2	Testing involves the use of a query language such as SQL, but no record and playback tool is being used.
4	No test tools are available.

Figure: Test tools

5) Environmental factor E =	
test tools	2
Development testing	8
test basis	3
development environm	2
test environment	1
testware	4

Test environment	
Rating	Description
1	The environment has been used for testing several times in the past.
2	The test is to be conducted in a newly equipped environment similar to other well-used environment within the organization.
4	The test is to be conducted in a newly equipped environment which may be considered experimental within the organization.

Figure: Test environment

5) Environmental factor E =		Test basis	
test tools	2	Rating	Description
Development testing	8	3	During the system development documentation standards are being used and a template, in addition the inspections are organized.
test basis	3		
development environm	2	6	During the system development documentation standards are being used and a template.
test environment	1		
testware	4	12	The system documentation was not developed using a specific standards and a template.

Figure: Test basis

5) Environmental factor E =		Development testing	
test tools	2	Rating	Description
Development testing	8	2	A development testing plan is available and the test team is familiar with the actual test cases and test results.
test basis	3		
development environm	2	4	A development testing plan is available.
test environment	1		
testware	4	8	No development testing plan is available.

Figure: Development testing

5) Environmental factor E =		Development environment	
test tools	2	Rating	Description
Development testing	8	2	The system was developed using a 4 GL programming language with an integrated DBMS containing numerous constraints.
test basis	3		
development environm	2	4	The system was developed using a 4 GL programming language, possibly in combination with a 3GL programming language.
test environment	1		
testware	4	8	The system was developed using only a 3 GL programming language such as COBOL, PASCAL OR PRG.

Figure: Development environment

Step 9 Calculate primary test hours (PT):

Primary test hours are the product of Test points, Skill factor and Environmental factors. Below formulae shows the concept in more detail:

$$Primary\ test\ hours = TP * Skill\ factor * E$$

For the accounting application total primary test hours are 101.73 as shown in the figure below.

6) Primary test hours (PT=TP*Skill*E)					
Skill factor	1.50				
PT=	71.21	*	1.50	*	0.95
TOTAL PRIMARY HOURS					**101.73**

Figure: Primary test hours

Step 10 Calculate total hours:

Every process involves planning and management activities also. We also need to take in to account these activities. Planning and management is affected by two important concepts Team size and Management tools. So below are the rating sheet for Team size and Management tools. These but values are summed and the percentage of this value is then multiplied with the primary test hours.

7) Total number of test hours		Team size	
		Rating	**Description**
Team size	3	3	The team consists of no more than four people.
Planning and control tools	8	6	The team consists of between five and ten people.
	11 %		
TOTAL HOURS		12	The team consists of more than ten people.

Figure: Number of test hours

7) Total number of test hours		Planning and control tools	
		Rating	**Description**
Team size	3	2	Both an automated time registration system and an automated defect tracking system (including CM) are available.
Planning and control tools	8		
	11 %	4	Either an automated time registration system or an automated defect tracking system (including CM) arte available.
TOTAL HOURS			
		8	No automated (management) systems are available.

Figure: Planning and control tools

Finally we distribute the same across the phases. So the total black box testing for this project in man is 101.73 man hours which 13 man day approximately.

8) Distribution over phases			Incl man.overhead		Excl man.overhead	
preparation	10	%	11.29	hour	10.17	hour
specification	40	%	45.17	hour	40.69	hour
execution	45	%	50.81	hour	45.78	hour
completion	5	%	5.65	hour	5.09	hour

Figure: Distribution over phases

(l)   Can you explain Number of defects measure?

> **Note:** *This question will be asked to measure what defects had you tracked from testing metrication perspective.*

Number of defects is one of the measures used to measure test effectiveness. One of the side effects of number of defects is that all bugs are not equal. So it becomes necessary to weight bugs according to there criticality level. If we using Number of defects as the metric measurement following are the issues:

·   Number of bugs that originally existed significantly impacts the number of bugs discovered, which in turns gives a wrong measure of the software quality.

·   All defects are not equal so defect should be numbered with criticality level to get the right software quality measure.

Below are three simple tables which show number of defects SDLC phase wise, module wise and developer wise.

Phase	Number of Defects		
	High	Medium	Low
Requirement	10	6	20
Design	7	8	9
Execution	4	3	2
Production	10	12	6

Figure: Number of defects phase wise

Modules	Number of Defects		
	High	Low	Medium
Cash Screen	7	5	4
Reports	10	12	8
Voucher Module	6	8	10
Login screen	12	3	4

Figure: Number of defects module wise.

Engineer	Number of Defects		
	High	Medium	Low
Vinod	15	9	4
Ravi	8	5	2
Ankit	6	3	1
Pradeep	11	7	6

Figure: Number of defects

(I)   Can you explain number of production defects measure?

This is one of the most effective measure. Number of defects found in production or the customer is recorded. The only issue with this measure is it can have latent and masked defects which can give us wrong value regarding software quality.

(I)   Can you explain defect seeding?

Defect seeding is a technique that was developed to estimate the number of defects resident in a piece of software. It's a bit offline technique and should not be used by every one. The process is the following we inject the application with defects and the see if the defect is found or not. So for instance if we have injected 100 defects we try to get three values first how many seeded defects where discovered, how many were not discovered and how many new defects (unseeded) are discovered. By using defect seeding we can predict the number of defect remaining in the system.

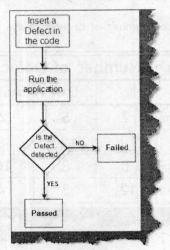

Figure: Defect seeding

Let's understand the concept of defect seeding by doing some detail calculation and also try to understand how we can predict the number of defects remaining in a system. Below is the calculation for the same.

- First calculate the seed ratio using the below given formulae i.e. Number of seed bugs found divided by total number of seeded bugs.
- After that we need to calculate the total number of defect by using the formulae Number of defects divided by seed ratio.
- Finally we can know the estimated defects by using the formulae Total number of defects – Number of defect calculated by step 3.

Below figure shows a sample with step by step calculation. You can see first we calculate the seed ratio, then total number of defects and finally we get the estimated defects.

$$\text{Seed Ratio} = \frac{\text{number of Seed Bugs Found}}{\text{Total number of Seed Bugs}}$$

number of Seed Bugs Found = **30**

Total number of Seed Bugs = **70**

$$\text{Seed Ratio} = \frac{30}{70} = 0.42 = 42\%$$

$$\text{Total number of Defects} = \frac{\text{number of Defects Found}}{\text{Seed Ratio}}$$

number of Defects Found = **160**

$$\text{Total number of Defects} = \frac{160}{0.42} = 380$$

Estimated **Defect** still present = **380 - 160** = **220**

Figure: Seed calculation

(I)   Can you explain DRE?

DRE(defect removal efficiency) is a powerful metric to measure test effectiveness. From this metric we come to know how many bugs we found out from the set of bugs which we could have found. Below is the formula for calculating DRE. So we need two inputs for calculating this metric number of bugs found during development and number of defects detected at the end user.

$$DRE = \frac{\text{Number of Bugs while Testing}}{\begin{array}{cc}\text{Number of Bugs} & \text{Number of Bugs}\\ \text{while Testing} & + \quad \text{found by User}\end{array}}$$

Number of Bugs while Testing = Bugs found during Development process while testing it.
Number of Bugs found by User = These are the Defect detected by the end-user.

Figure:DRE formulae

But success of DRE depends on lot of factors. Below are listed some factors:

·   Severity and distribution of bugs must be taken in to account.
·   Second how do we confirm when the customer has found all the bugs. This is normally achieved by looking at the past history of the customer.

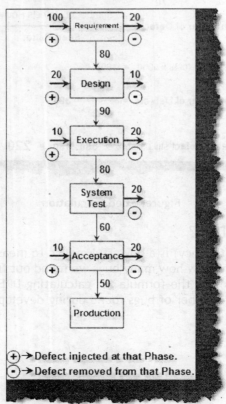

Figure: Defect injected and removed per phase

(B) Can you explain Unit and system test DRE?

DRE is also useful to measure effectiveness of a particular test like acceptance, unit or system testing. Below figure shows defect numbers at various software cycle level. The + indicates that defects are input to the phase and - indicates that these many defects where removed from that particular phase. For instance in requirement phase 100 defects where present, but 20 defects are removed from the requirement phase due to code review. So if 20 defects are removed then 80 defects get carried to the new phase (design) and so on.

First let's calculate simple DRE of the above diagram. DRE will be total bugs found in testing divided by total bugs found in testing plus total bugs found by user that is during acceptance testing. So below diagram gives the DRE for the above values.

$$DRE = \frac{\text{Number of Bugs while Testing}}{\text{Number of Bugs while Testing} + \text{Number of Bugs found by User}}$$

$$= \frac{(20 + 10 + 20 + 20 + 20)}{(20 + 10 + 20 + 20 + 20) + 50}$$

$$= \frac{(90)}{(90) + 50}$$

$$= \frac{90}{140} = 0.64\%$$

Figure: DRE calculation

Now lets calculate system DRE of the above given project. In order to calculate the system DRE we need to take number of defects found during system divided by defects found during system testing plus defects found during acceptance testing. Below figure shows the System DRE calculation in a step by step fashion.

$$\text{System Test DRE} = \frac{\text{Number of Bugs during System Testing}}{\begin{array}{c}\text{Number of Bugs} \\ \text{during} \\ \text{System Testing}\end{array} + \begin{array}{c}\text{Number of Bugs} \\ \text{found during} \\ \text{Acceptance Testing}\end{array}}$$

$$= \frac{20}{20 + 20}$$

$$= \frac{20}{40}$$

$$\text{System Test DRE} = 0.5\%$$

Figure: System test DRE calculation

Unit testing DRE calculation will be similar to system testing DRE. As you can see from the below figure its nothing but Number of defects found during Unit testing divided by Number of defects found during unit testing plus Number of defects found during system testing.

$$\text{Unit Test DRE} = \frac{\text{Number of Bugs during Unit Testing}}{\begin{array}{c}\text{Number of Bugs} \\ \text{during} \\ \text{Unit Testing}\end{array} + \begin{array}{c}\text{Number of Bugs} \\ \text{found during} \\ \text{System Testing}\end{array}}$$

$$= \frac{20}{20 + 20}$$

$$= \frac{20}{40}$$

$$\text{Unit Test DRE} = 0.5\%$$

Figure: Unit test DRE calculation

One of the important factors to be noted while calculating unit test DRE is that we need to exclude those defects which can not produced due to limitation of unit testing. For instance passing of data between components to other. In unit testing because we test it as a single unit we can never reproduce defects which involves interaction. So such kind of defects which can not be produced due to the nature of the testing itself should be removed to get accurate test results.

(I)   How do you measure test effectiveness?

Test effectiveness is measure of the bug finding ability of our tests. In short it **measures** how good the tests were?. So effectiveness is the ratio of measure of bugs found **during** testing to total bugs found. Total bugs are the sum of new defects found by user + **bugs** found in test. Below figure explains the calculation in a more pictorial format.

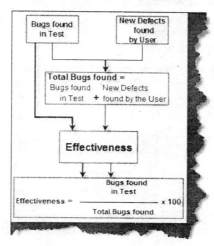

Figure: Measure test effectiveness

(B)   Can you explain Defect age and Defect spoilage?

Defect age is also called as Phase Age or Phage. One of the most important things to remember in testing is later we find a defect more it costs to fix. Defect age and Defects spoilage metrics works on the same fundamental i.e. how late you found the defect? So the first thing we need to define is what is the scale of the defect age according to phases. For instance the below table defines the scale according to the Phases. So for instance requirement defects if found in design phase has a scale of 1 and the same defect if propagated till the production phase goes up to a scale of 4.

Phase created	Requirement	Design	Execution	Testing	Production
Requirement	0	1	2	3	4
Design	0	0	1	2	3
Execution	0	0	0	1	2

Figure: Scale of Defect Age

Once the scale is decided now we can find the defect spoilage. Defect spoilage is defects from the previous phase multiplied by the scale. For instance in the below figure we have found 8 defects in the design phase from which 4 defects are propagated from the requirement phase. So we multiply the 4 defects with the scale defined in the previous table, so we get the value of 4. In the same fashion we calculate for all the phases. Below given is the spoilage formula. It's the ratio of sum of defects passed from the previous phase multiplied by the discovered phase then finally divided by the total number of defects. For instance the first row shows that total defects are 27 and sum of passed on defects multiplied by their factor is 8 (4 x 1 = 4 + 2 x 2 = 4). In this way we calculate for all phases and finally the total. The optimal value is 1. Lower value of spoilage indicates more effective defect discovery process.

Phase Created	Requirement	Design	Execution	Testing	Production	Total
Requirement	0	Def = 8 (1) Req Def = 4 4 x 1 = 4	Def = 10 (2) Req Def = 2 2 x 2 = 4	Def = 9 (3) Req Def = 0	(4) --	$\frac{8}{27}$ = 0.29
Design	0	0	Def = 4 (1) Des. Def = 5 5 x 1 = 5	Def = 2 (2) Des. Def = 3 3 x 2 = 6	Def = 0 (3) Des. Def = 1 1 x 3 = 3	$\frac{14}{6}$ = 2.33
Execution	0	0	0	Def = 4 (1) Exec.Def= 2 2 x 1 = 2	Def = 0 (2) Exec.Def= 0	$\frac{2}{4}$ = 0.5
Main Total	NA	NA	NA	NA	NA	$\frac{24}{37}$ = 0.64

Figure: Defect Spoilage

$$\text{Spoilage} = \frac{\text{sum of number of Defects x Discovered Phage}}{\text{Total number of Defects}}$$

Figure: Spoilage formulae

6

CMMI

(B) What is a Software process?

A process is a series of step to solve a problem. Below figure shows a pictorial view of how an organization has defined a way to solve any risk problem. In the below diagram we have shown two branches one is what exactly is a process and the second branch shows a sample risk mitigation process for an organization. For instance the below risk mitigation process defines what step any department should follow to mitigate a risk.

· Identify the risk of the project by discussion, proper requirement gathering and forecasting.

· Once you have identified the risk prioritize which risk has the most impact and should be tackled on priority basis.

· Analyze how the risk can be solved by proper impact analysis and planning.

· Finally using the above analysis we mitigate the risk.

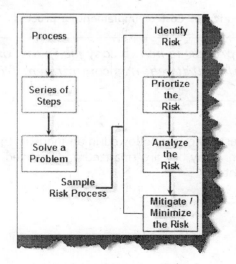

Figure: Software Process

(I) What are the different cost element involved in implementing process in an organization?

Below is some of the cost elements involved in implementing process:

- **Salary**: This forms the major component of implementing any process salary of the employees. Normally while implementing process in a company either organization can recruit full time guys or they can share a resource part time on implementing the process.
- **Consultant**: If the process is new it can also involve in taking consultants which is again an added cost.
- **Training Cost**: Employee of the company also have to undergo training in order to implement the new process.
- **Tools**: In order to implement process organization will also need to buy tools which again need to be budgeted.

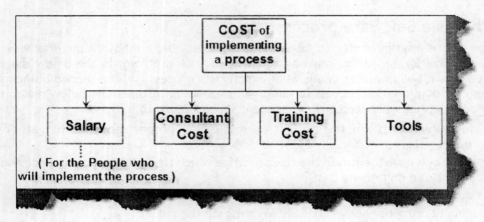

Figure: Cost of implementing process

> **Note:** *Implementing a process is not an easy job in any organization. More than financial commitment it requires commitment from people to follow the process.*

(B) What is a model?

Model is nothing but best practices followed in an industry to solve issues and problems. Models are not made in a day but are finalized and realized by years of experience and continuous improvements.

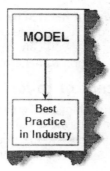

Figure: Model

Many companies reinvent the wheel rather than following already time tested models in industry.

(B) What is maturity level?

Maturity level specifies the level of performance expected from the organization.

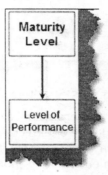

Figure: Maturity level

(B) Can you explain the concept of process area in CMMI?

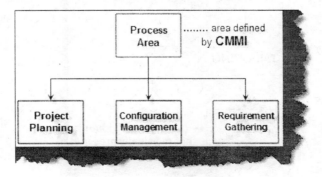

Figure: Process Area in action

Process area is the area of improvement defined by CMMI. Every maturity level consists of Process Areas. Process Area is a group of practice or activities performed collectively to achieve specific objective. For instance you can look in to below figure we have process areas like Project Planning, Configuration Management and Requirement gathering.

(B) Can you explain the concept of tailoring?

As the name specifies tailoring is nothing but changing the action to achieve objective according to conditions. Whenever tailoring is done there should be adequate reasons for why tailoring is done for that process. Remember when a process is defined in an organization it should be followed properly. So even if tailoring is applied the process is not bypassed or omitted.

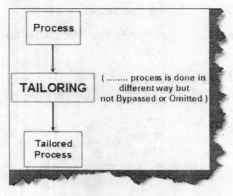

Figure: Tailoring

Let's try to understand this by a simple example. Let's say in a organization there is process defined that every contract should have a hard copy signed. But there can be scenarios in the organization when the person is not present physically, so for those scenarios the contract should be signed through email. So in short the process for signing a contract is not bypassed only the process approach is tailored.

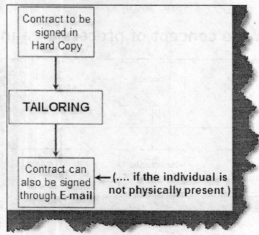

Figure: Example of tailoring

(B) What is CMMI?

> ***Note:*** *One of my seniors gave a very decent answer to what is CMMI in his own words. Here it goes how he explained me in his own words. There are two aspects of CMMI one is the capability and other is the maturity. He said it's possible that you are capable of drinking 10 bottles of wine, but after drinking 10 bottles of wine you fall sick. But it's your maturity that you can drink 10 bottle of wine, eat well and do not fall sick. I think this was the best answer I ever got about capability and maturity. Same applies for organization its your capability that you can complete a project with out quality, but its your maturity that you can complete project with proper quality implementation. By the way my favorite is VODKA fuel with mirinda and two ice J You know what guys I am matured enough so I eat a lot after drinking.*

CMMI stands for Capability Maturity Model Integration. It is a process improvement approach that provides companies with the essential elements of effective process. CMMI can serve as a good guide for process improvement across a project, organization or division.

CMMI was formed by using multiple previous CMM process. Below are the areas which CMMI addresses because of integrating with CMM process:

Systems engineering: This covers development of total systems. System engineers concentrate on converting customer needs to product solution and support them through out the product life cycle.

Software Engineering: Software engineers concentrate on the application of systematic, disciplined, and quantifiable approaches to the development, operation, and maintenance of software.

Integrated Product and Process Development: Integrated Product and Process Development (IPPD) is a systematic approach that achieves a timely collaboration of relevant stakeholders throughout the life of the product to better satisfy customer needs, expectations, and requirements. This section mostly concentrates on the integration part of the project for different processes. For instance it's possible that your project is using services of some other third party component. In such situation the integration is a big task itself and if approached in a systematic manner can be handled with ease.

Software Acquisition: Many times organization has to acquire products of other organization. Acquisition is itself a big step for any organization and if not handled in a proper manner means just calling for disaster.

Below is what CMMI call about.

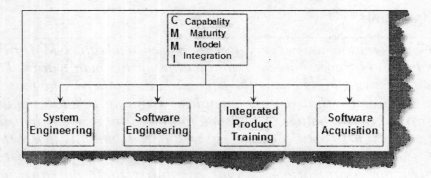

Figure: CMMI

(I) What's the difference between implementation and Institutionalization?

Both of these concepts are important while implementing process in any organization. Any new process implemented has to go through these two phases.

Implementation: It is just performing task within a process area (for definition of process area look in to the same chapter). Task is performed according to a process but actions performed to complete the process are not ingrained in the organization. That means the process involved is according to individual point of view. When an organization starts to implement any process it first starts at this phase i.e. Implementation and then when this process sounds good it is raised to the organization level so that it can be implemented across organizations.

Institutionalization: Institutionalization is the output of implementing the process again and again. The difference between implementation and institutionalization is in the implementation the person who implemented the process goes the process is not followed, but if the process is institutionalized then even if the person leaves the organization, the process is still followed.

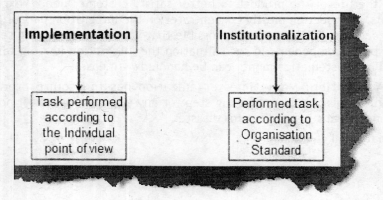

Figure: Implementation and Institutionalization

(I) What are different models in CMMI?

(I) Can you explain staged and continuous models in CMMI?

There are two aspects in CMMI one is the capability and other is the maturity. Capability means the ability to perform task while maturity means to perform task in a matured fashion. Both the CMMI models lie in of the above category. There are two models in CMMI first is "staged" in which maturity level organizes the process areas, second is "continuous" in which the capability level organize the process area.

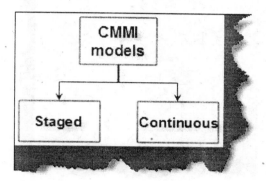

Figure: CMMI models

Below figure shows how process areas are grouped in both models.

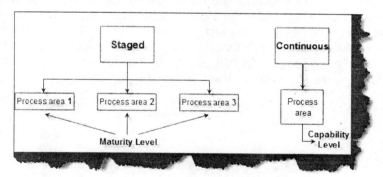

Figure: Staged and continuous models

Let's try to understand both the models in a more detail manner. Before we move ahead deeper in differences of the two models lets understand the basic structure of CMMI process, goal and practices. A process area as said previously is a group of practices or activities performed to achieve specific objective. Every process area has specific as well as generic goal that should be satisfied to achieve that objective. To achieve those goals we need to follow certain practices. So again to achieve those specific goals we have specific practices and to achieve generic goals we have generic practices.

In one of our previous questions we talked about implementation and Institutionalization. Implementation can be related to specific practice while Institutionalization can be related to generics practices. So this is what the common basic structure in both models Process area à Specific / Generic goals à Specific / Generic practice.

Now let's try to understand model structures with both types of representations. In staged representation we revolve around maturity level as shown in figure below. So all process have to be at one maturity level.

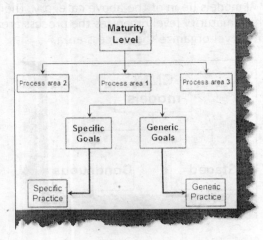

Figure: Staged representation

While in continuous representation we try to achieve capability levels in those practices. Below diagram shows how continuous representation revolves around capability. Continuous representation is used when the organization wants to mature and perform in one specific process area only. Let's say for instance in a non-it organization one wants to only improve its supplier agreement process. So that particular organization will only concentrate on SAM and try to achieve good capability level in that process area.

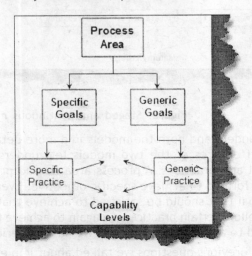

Figure: Continuous representation

(I) Can you explain the different maturity levels in staged representation?

There are five maturity levels in staged representation as shown in figure below.

Maturity Level 1(Initial): In this level everything is adhoc. Development is completely chaotic with budget and schedules often exceeded. In this scenario we can never predict quality and the project are run by heroes'. If the heroes go off the whole project goes for a toss.

Maturity Level 2 (Managed): In managed level basic project management are in place. But the basic project management and practices are followed only in the project level.

Maturity Level 3 (Defined): To reach this level the organization should have achieved first level 2. In the previous level the good practice and process was only done at project level. But in this level all these good practice and process is brought at the organization level. There are set and standard practice defined at the organization level which every project should follow. Maturity Level 3 moves ahead with defining a strong, meaningful, organization view approach to developing products. An important distinction between Maturity Levels 2 and 3 is that at Level 3, processes are described in more detail and more rigorously than at Level 2 and are at organization level.

Maturity Level 4 (Quantitively measured): To start with this level organization should have achieved Level 2 and Level3. In this level more of statistics comes in to picture. Organization controls its project by statistical and other quantitative techniques. Product quality, process performance, and service quality are understood in statistical terms and are managed throughout the life of the processes. Maturity Level 4 concentrates on using metrics to make decisions and to truly measure whether progress is happening and the product is becoming better. The main difference between Levels 3 and 4 are that at Level 3, processes are qualitatively predictable. At Level 4, processes are quantitatively predictable. Level 4 addresses causes of process variation and takes corrective action.

Maturity Level 5 (Optimized): The organization has achieved goals of Maturity Levels 2, 3, and 4. In this level Processes are continually improved, based on an understanding of common causes of variation within the processes. This is like the final level everyone in the team is a productive member, defects are minimized, and products are delivered on time and within the budget boundary.

Below figure shows in detail all the maturity levels in a pictorial fashion.

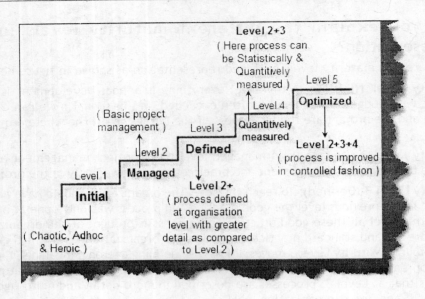

Figure: Maturity level in staged model

(I) Can you explain capability levels in continuous representation?

Continuous model is same as staged model only that the arrangement is bit different. Continuous representation / model concentrate on the action or task to be completed within a process area. It focuses on maturing the organization ability to perform, control and improve the performance in that specific performance area.

Capability Level 0: Incomplete

This level means that any generic or specific practice of Capability level 1 is not performed.

Capability Level 1: Performed

Capability level 1 process is expected to perform all capability level 1 specific and generic practices for that process area. In this level performance may not be stable and probably does not meet objectives like quality, cost and schedule, but yes still the task can be done. It's a first step, it's like you are doing the process but you can not really prove it if it's the most effective.

Capability Level 2: Managed

A managed process planned properly, performed, monitored, and controlled to achieve a given purpose. Because the process is managed we achieve other objectives, such as cost, schedule, and quality. Because you are managing some metrics are consistently collected and applied to your management approach.

Capability Level 3: Defined

Defined process is a managed process that is tailored from organization standard. Tailoring is done by justification and documentation guidelines. So for instance your organization has a standard that we should take invoice from every supplier. But for any instance if the supplier is not able to supply the invoice then he should sign an agreement and give in place of the invoice. So here the invoice standard is not followed but the deviation is under control.

Capability Level 4: Qua.ititatively Managed

Quantitatively Managed process is a defined process which is controlled through statistical and quantitative information. So right from defect tracking, to project schedules are all statistically tracked and measured for that process.

Capability Level 5: Optimizing

Optimizing process is a quantitatively managed process where we increase process performance through incremental and innovative improvements.

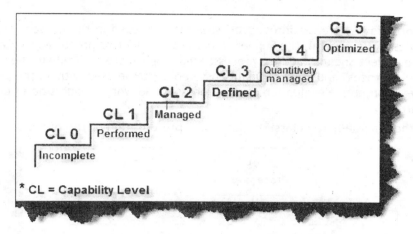

Figure: Capability levels in continuous model

If you really see continuous representation is same as the staged only that information is arranged in a different fashion. The biggest difference is one concentrates on a specific process while the other brings a groups of process to a certain mature levels.

(I) Which model should we use and under what scenarios?

Staging defines an organization process implementation sequence. So staging is a sequence of targeted process areas that describe a path of process improvement the organization will take. For instance you can not do your project planning (Level 2) if you have not done requirements management (Level 2). While in continuous you select certain process area irrespective even if it's linked with other process area and mature in that.

So when you want that your organization should only concentrate on specific process areas you will like to go for continuous model. But if you want that you want to that your organization should have a specific plan and should not only achieve in the specific process but also any interlinked process with that process area you should go for staged.

(A) How many process areas are present in CMMI and in what classification do they fall in?

All 25 process areas in CMMI are classified inside four major sections. Process management

This process areas contain the across project tasks related to defining, planning, executing, implementing, monitoring, controlling, measuring, and making better processes.

Project management

Project Management process areas cover the project management activities related to planning, monitoring, and controlling the project.

Engineering

The Engineering process areas were written using general engineering terminology so that any technical discipline involved in the product development process (e.g., software engineering or mechanical engineering) can use them for process improvement.

Support

The Support process areas address processes that are used in the context of performing other processes. In general, the Support process areas address processes that are targeted toward the project and may address processes that apply more generally to the organization. For example, Process and Product Quality Assurance can be used with all the process areas to provide an objective evaluation of the processes and work products described in all the process areas.

Below is the diagrammatic classification and representation of the process areas.

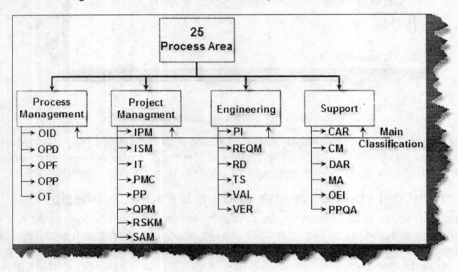

Figure: 25 Process Area

Below table defines all the abbreviation of the process areas.

Abbreviation for 25 Process area : -			
Process Management		**Engineering**	
OID	Organisational Innovation & Deployment	PI	Product Integration
OPD	Organisational Process Definition	REQM	Requirements Management
OPF	Organisational Process Focus	RD	Requirements Development
OPP	Organisational Process Performance	TS	Technical Solution
OT	Organisational Training	VAL	Validation
		VER	Verification
Project Management		**Support**	
IPM	Integrated Project Management	CAR	Casual Analysis & Resolution
ISM	Integrated Supplier Management	CM	Configuration Management
IT	Integrated Teaming	DAR	Decision Analysis & Resolution
PMC	Project Monitoring & Control	MA	Measurement & Analysis
PP	Project Planning	OEI	Organisational Environment for Integration
QPM	Quantitative Project Management	PPQA	Process & Product Quality Assurance
RSKM	Risk Management		
SAM	Supplier Management Agreement		

Figure: Abbreviation of all process areas

(B) What the difference between every level in CMMI?

Level 1 and Level 2:

This is the biggest steps for any organization. Because the organization moves from a immature position to a more mature organization. Level l is adhoc process in which people have created personal process to accomplish certain task. With this approach there is lot of redundant work and people do not share their information also. This leads to heroes' in the project, so when people out of the organization the knowledge also moves out and organization suffers.

In maturity level 2 individual share their lesson and best practices, which leads to devising preliminary process at project and in some cases it also moves to organization level. In level 2 we focus on project management issues that affect day to day routine. It has seven process areas as shown in figure below.

So in short difference between level 1 and level 2 is of immature and mature organization.

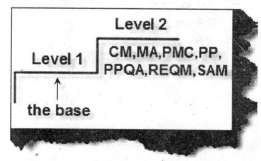

Figure: From level 1 to Level 2

Level 2 to Level 3:

Now that in Level 2 good practices are practiced at project level it is time to move these good practices to organization level so that every one is benefited from the same. So the biggest difference between Level 2 and Level 3 is good practices from the projects are bubbled up to organization level. Organization approach of doing business is documented. To perform Maturity level 3 first Maturity 2 should be achieved with the 14 process as shown in the given figure.

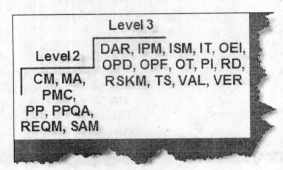

Figure: Level 2 to Level 3

Level 3 to Level 4:

Maturity level 4 is all about numbers and statistics. All aspects of the project are managed by numbers. All decisions are made by numbers. Product quality and process are measured by numbers. So in Level 3 we if we say this is good in quality, in Level 4 we say this is good in quality because the defect ratio is less than 1 %. So there two process areas in Level 4 as shown below. In order to Level 4 you should have achieved all the PA's of Level 3 and also the below two process areas.

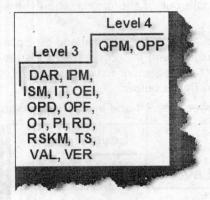

Figure: Level 3 to Level 4

Level 4 to Level 5:

Level 5 is all about improvement as compared to Level 4. Level 5 concentrates on improving quality of organization process by identifying variation, by looking at root causes of the conditions and incorporating improvements for improve process. Below are the two process areas in Level 5 as shown in figure below. In order to get level 5 all level 4 PA's should be satisfied. So the basic difference between level 4 and level 5 is in Level 4 we have already achieved a good level of quality, and in level 5 we are trying to improve the quality.

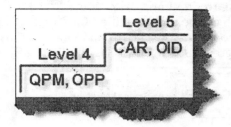

Figure: Level 4 to Level 5

(I) What different sources are needed to verify authenticity for CMMI implementation?

There are three different sources from which an appraiser can verify that did the organization follow process or not.

Instruments: It is a survey or questionnaire provided to the organization, project or individuals before starting the assessment. So that before hand appraiser knows some basic details of the project.

Interview: It's a formal meeting between one or more members of the organization in which they are asked some questions and the appraiser makes some judgments based on those interviews. During the interview the member represents some process areas or role which he performs in context of those process areas. For instance the appraiser may interview a tester or programmer asking him indirectly what metrics he has submitted to his project manager. By this the appraiser gets a fair idea of CMMI implementation in that organization.

Documents: It's a written work or product which serves as an evidence that a process is followed. It can be hard copy, word document, email or any type of written official proof.

Below is the pictorial view of sources to verify how much compliant the organization is with CMMI.

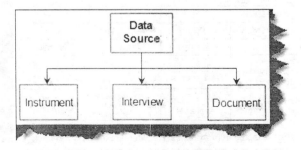

Figure: Different data source for verification

(I)   Can you explain SCAMPI process?

(I)   How is appraisal done in CMMI?

SCAMPI stands for Standard CMMI Appraisal Method for Process Improvement. SCAMPI is an assessment process to get be CMMI certified for a organization. There are three classes of CMMI appraisal methods class A, class B and class C. Class A is the most aggressive, while Class B is less aggressive and Class C is the least aggressive.

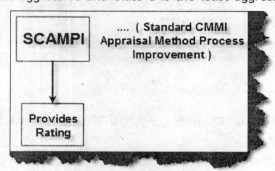

Figure: SCAMPI

Let's discuss all these appraisal methods in more detail.

Class A: This is the only method that can provide rating and get you a CMMI certificate. It requires all three sources of data instruments, interview and documents.

Class B: This requires only two sources of data (interviews and either documents or instruments). But please note you do not get rated with Class B appraisals. Class B is just a warm up that if the organization is ready for Class A. With less verification the appraisal takes less time. In this data sufficiency and draft presentation are optional.

Class .C: It requires only one source of data (interview, instruments or documents). Team consensus, validation; observation, data sufficiency, and draft presentation are optional.

Below table shows the characteristic features with proper comparison.

Characteristic	Class A	Class B	Class C
Amount of objective evidence gathered (relative)	High	Medium	Low
Rating generated	Yes	No	No
Resource needs (relative)	High	Medium	Low
Team size (relative)	Large	Medium	Small
Data sources (instruments, interview, & documents)	Requires all 3 Data sources	Requires 2 Data sources one must be Interview	Requires only 1 Data sources
Appraisal Team Leader requirement	Authorized Lead Appraiser	Authorized Lead Appraiser or person trained & experienced	Person trained & experienced

* **Source:** adapted from Appraisal Requirement for CMMI Version 1.1

Figure: Comparison between Class A, B and C

(I)   Which appraisal method class is the best?

Normally organizations use mix breed of the classes to achieve process improvement. Below are some of the strategies which organization use:

First Strategy

Use class B to initiate process improvement plan. After that apply Class C to see readiness for Class B or Class A. Below diagram shows the strategy.

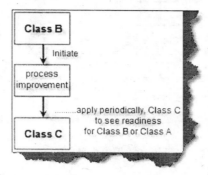

Figure: Strategy one

Second strategy

Class C appraisal is used on subset of organization. From this we get aggregation of weakness across organization. From this we can prepare process improvement plan. We can then apply Class B appraisal to see that are we ready for Class A appraisal. Below diagram shows the strategy.

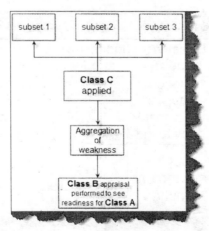

Figure: Second strategy

Third Strategy

Class A is used to initiate organization level process. The process improvement plan is based on identified weakness. Class B appraisal should be performed after six months to see the readiness for second class A appraisal rating. Below diagram shows the strategy.

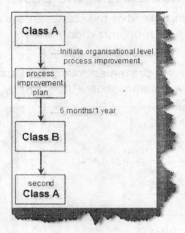

Figure: Third Strategy

(l)   Can you explain the importance of PII in SCAMPI?

Using PII i.e. Practice implementation indicators we take information about the organization. PII gives us a compliance matrix showing how practices are performed in organization. PII basically consists of three types of information direct work product, indirect work product and affirmations. Direct work product and indirect work product come from document while affirmations come from interviews. The below table shows a sample PIID information for process SAM and for one of the key process areas.

SG 1 : - Establish Supplier Agreement		
PII Type	Direct work products	Indirect work products	Affirmation
Organisation Evidence	signed supplier agreement copy found	supplier agreement document was used to pass invoices	supplier has to sign supplier agreement
Notes	supplier agreement found	invoices passed with supplier agreement	

Figure: Sample PIID

Once the PIID are filled we can rate saying is the organization compliant or not. So below are the steps to be followed during the SCAMPI:

- Gather documentation.
- Conduct interviews.
- Discover and document strengths and weaknesses.
- Communicate / present findings.

(A) Can you explain implementation of CMMI in one of the Key process areas?

> **Note:** *This question will be asked to judge whether you have actually implemented CMMI in a proper fashion in your oganization or not. For answering this question we will be using SAM as the process area. But you can answer with whatever process area you have implemented in your organization.*

For SAM below are the two SG1 and SG2 practice which needs to be implemented to satisfy the process area. SAM helps us to define our agreement with Supplier while procuring products in the company. Let's see in the next step how we have mapped our existing process with SAM practices defined in CMMI.

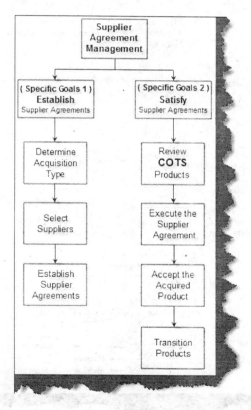

Figure: SAM process area

In order to specify SAM below is a process adopted by the company. If any body wants to demand any product he has to first raise demand for the item by using the demand form which is defined by the company. Depending on demand the supervisor defines which acquisition type is this demand. For instance is it a production acquisition type, office material acquisition type or others. Once the acquisition type is decided the organization places an advertisement in the news paper to ask suppliers for quotation. Once all quotations are received depending on cost, quality and other factors final supplier is decided. Supplier is then called to the office and he has to sign an agreement with the organization for the delivery of the product. Once the agreement is signed supplier sends a sample product which is analyzed by the organization practically. Finally the product is accepted and supplier is then asked to send the complete delivery of all products. The product is accepted in the organization by issuing the supplier a proper invoice. The invoice document says that the product is accepted by the organization officially. When the product is installed in the organization then either someone from the supplier side comes for the demo or a help brochure is shipped with the product.

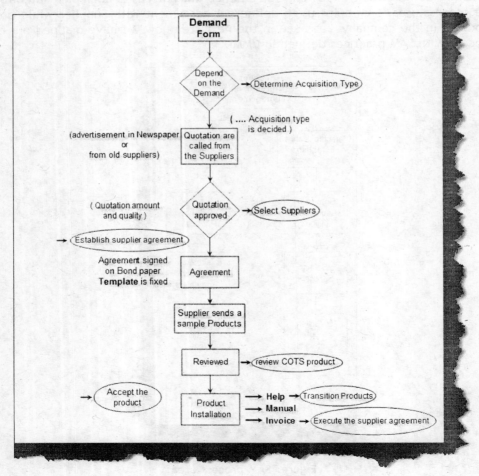

Figure: SAM process area mapped with actual world

Ok now the above explanation was from the perspective of the how the organization managed its transaction with the suppliers. Now let's try to map how the above process fits in CMMI model. In the above diagram all the circled description is nothing but process areas of CMMI.

CMMI process	Organization process
Determine Acquisition type	In the above process Demand form decides what the Acquisition type of the product is.
Select suppliers	Looking at the quotation the supplier is review and the selection is done.
Establish Supplier agreements	In the above process we have a step when we sign agreement with the supplier which establishes all the terms and conditions for the supplier agreement.
Review Product	One of the step of the process is that supplier has to send a sample which is reviewed by the organization.
Execute Supplier agreements	Supplier agreement is executed by accepting invoice.
Accept Acquired product	Invoice is the proof for acceptance of the product.
Transition products	In the above process the transition of the product either happens through help brochures or when the demo person visits he gives a KT.

(B) Explanation of all process areas with goals and practices?

(A) Can you explain the process areas?

Note: *No one is going to ask such a question. But they would like to know at least the purpose of each KPA. Second they would like to know what you did to attain compatibility to these process areas. For instance you say that you did Organizational Process Definition. They would like to know how you did it. For instance you can justify it by saying that you made standard documents for coding standards which was then followed at the organization level for reference. Normally every one follows process it's only that they do not know. So try to map the KPA to the process what you follow. The only purpose to paste all the KPA is if in case you are looking for some higher positions in big companies they really expect you to speak in term of KPA rather than generic term. This whole stuff can be like a quick reference for you before entering the interview room.*

Each process area is defined by a set of goals and practices. There are two categories of goals and practices: generic and specific. Generic goals and practices are a part of every process area. Specific goals and practices are specific to a given process area. A process area is satisfied when company processes cover all of the generic and specific goals and practices for that process area.

Generic goals and practices

Generic goals and practices are a part of every process area.

> GG 1 Achieve Specific Goals
>
> GP 1.1 Perform Base Practices
>
> GG 2 Institutionalize a Managed Process
>
> GP 2.1 Establish an Organizational Policy
>
> GP 2.2 Plan the Process
>
> GP 2.3 Provide Resources
>
> GP 2.4 Assign Responsibility
>
> GP 2.5 Train People
>
> GP 2.6 Manage Configurations
>
> GP 2.7 Identify and Involve Relevant Stakeholders
>
> GP 2.8 Monitor and Control the Process
>
> GP 2.9 Objectively Evaluate Adherence
>
> GP 2.10 Review Status with Higher Level Management
>
> GG 3 Institutionalize a Defined Process
>
> GP 3.1 Establish a Defined Process
>
> GP 3.2 Collect Improvement Information
>
> GG 4 Institutionalize a Quantitatively Managed Process
>
> GP 4.1 Establish Quantitative Objectives for the Process
>
> GP 4.2 Stabilize Sub process Performance
>
> GG 5 Institutionalize an Optimizing Process
>
> GP 5.1 Ensure Continuous Process Improvement
>
> GP 5.2 Correct Root Causes of Problems

Process areas

The CMMI contains 25 key process areas indicating the aspects of product development that are to be covered by company processes.

Causal Analysis and Resolution (CAR)

A Support process area at Maturity Level 5

Purpose

The purpose of Causal Analysis and Resolution (CAR) is to identify causes of defects and other problems and take action to prevent them from occurring in the future.

Specific Practices by Goal

> SG 1 Determine Causes of Defects
>
> SP 1.1-1 Select Defect Data for Analysis
>
> SP 1.2-1 Analyze Causes
>
> SG 2 Address Causes of Defects

SP 2.1-1 Implement the Action Proposals

SP 2.2-1 Evaluate the Effect of Changes

SP 2.3-1 Record Data

Configuration Management (CM)

A Support process area at Maturity Level 2

Purpose

The purpose of Configuration Management (CM) is to establish and maintain the integrity of work products using configuration identification, configuration control, configuration status accounting, and configuration audits.

Specific Practices by Goal

SG 1 Establish Baselines

SP 1.1-1 Identify Configuration Items

SP 1.2-1 Establish a Configuration Management System

SP 1.3-1 Create or Release Baselines

SG 2 Track and Control Changes

SP 2.1-1 Track Change Requests

SP 2.2-1 Control Configuration Items

SG 3 Establish Integrity

SP 3.1-1 Establish Configuration Management Records

SP 3.2-1 Perform Configuration Audits

Decision Analysis and Resolution (DAR)

A Support process area at Maturity Level 3

Purpose

The purpose of Decision Analysis and Resolution (DAR) is to analyze possible decisions using a formal evaluation process that evaluates identified alternatives against established criteria.

Specific Practices by Goal

SG 1 Evaluate Alternatives

SP 1.1-1 Establish Guidelines for Decision Analysis

SP 1.2-1 Establish Evaluation Criteria

SP 1.3-1 Identify Alternative Solutions

SP 1.4-1 Select Evaluation Methods

SP 1.5-1 Evaluate Alternatives

SP 1.6-1 Select Solutions

Integrated Project Management (IPM)

A Project Management process area at Maturity Level 3

Purpose

The purpose of Integrated Project Management (IPM) is to establish and manage the project and the involvement of the relevant stakeholders according to an integrated and defined process that is tailored from the organization's set of standard processes.

Specific Practices by Goal

SG 1 Use the Project's Defined Process

SP 1.1-1 Establish the Project's Defined Process

SP 1.2-1 Use Organizational Process Assets for Planning Project Activities

SP 1.3-1 Integrate Plans

SP 1.4-1 Manage the Project Using the Integrated Plans

SP 1.5-1 Contribute to the Organizational Process Assets

SG 2 Coordinate and Collaborate with Relevant Stakeholders

SP 2.1-1 Manage Stakeholder Involvement

SP 2.2-1 Manage Dependencies

SP 2.3-1 Resolve Coordination Issues

SG 3 Use the Project's Shared Vision for IPPD

SP 3.1-1 Define Project's Shared Vision for IPPD

SP 3.2-1 Establish the Project's Shared Vision

SG 4 Organize Integrated Teams for IPPD

SP 4.1-1 Determine Integrated Team Structure for the Project

SP 4.2-1 Develop a Preliminary Distribution of Requirements to Integrated Teams

SP 4.3-1 Establish Integrated Teams

Integrated Supplier Management (ISM)

A Project Management process area at Maturity Level 3

Purpose

The purpose of Integrated Supplier Management (ISM) is to proactively identify sources of products that may be used to satisfy the project's requirements and to manage selected suppliers while maintaining a cooperative project-supplier relationship.

Specific Practices by Goal

SG 1 Analyze and Select Sources of Products

SP 1.1-1 Analyze Potential Sources of Products

SP 1.2-1 Evaluate and Determine Sources of Products

SG 2 Coordinate Work with Suppliers

SP 2.1-1 Monitor Selected Supplier Processes

SP 2.2-1 Evaluate Selected Supplier Work Products

SP 2.3-1 Revise the Supplier Agreement or Relationship

Integrated Teaming (IT)

A Project Management process area at Maturity Level 3

Purpose

The purpose of Integrated Teaming (IT) is to form and sustain an integrated team for the development of work products.

Specific Practices by Goal

SG 1 Establish Team Composition

SP 1.1-1 Identify Team Tasks

SP 1.2-1 Identify Needed Knowledge and Skills

SP 1.3-1 Assign Appropriate Team Members

SG 2 Govern Team Operation

SP 2.1-1 Establish a Shared Vision

SP 2.2-1 Establish a Team Charter

SP 2.3-1 Define Roles and Responsibilities

SP 2.4-1 Establish Operating Procedures

SP 2.5-1 Collaborate among Interfacing Teams

Measurement and Analysis (MA)

A Support process area at Maturity Level 2

Purpose

The purpose of Measurement and Analysis (MA) is to develop and sustain a measurement capability that is used to support management information needs.

Specific Practices by Goal

SG 1 Align Measurement and Analysis Activities

SP 1.1-1 Establish Measurement Objectives

SP 1.2-1 Specify Measures SP 1.3-1 Specify Data Collection and Storage Procedures

SP 1.4-1 Specify Analysis Procedures

SG 2 Provide Measurement Results

SP 2.1-1 Collect Measurement Data

SP 2.2-1 Analyze Measurement Data

SP 2.3-1 Store Data and Results

SP 2.4-1 Communicate Results

Organizational Environment for Integration (OEI)

A Support process area at Maturity Level 3

Purpose

The purpose of Organizational Environment for Integration (OEI) is to provide an Integrated Product and Process Development (IPPD) infrastructure and manage people for integration.

Specific Practices by Goal

SG 1 Provide IPPD Infrastructure

SP 1.1-1 Establish the Organization's Shared Vision

SP 1.2-1 Establish an Integrated Work Environment

SP 1.3-1 Identify IPPD-Unique Skill Requirements

SG 2 Manage People for Integration

SP 2.1-1 Establish Leadership Mechanisms

SP 2.2-1 Establish Incentives for Integration

SP 2.3-1 Establish Mechanisms to Balance Team and Home Organization Responsibilities

Organizational Innovation and Deployment (OID)

A Process Management process area at Maturity Level 5

Purpose

The purpose of Organizational Innovation and Deployment (OID) is to select and deploy incremental and innovative improvements that measurably improve the organization's processes and technologies. The improvements support the organization's quality and process-performance objectives as derived from the organization's business objectives.

Specific Practices by Goal

SG 1 Select Improvements

SP 1.1-1 Collect and Analyze Improvement Proposals

SP 1.2-1 Identify and Analyze Innovations

SP 1.3-1 Pilot Improvements

SP 1.4-1 Select Improvements for Deployment

SG 2 Deploy Improvements

SP 2.1-1 Plan the Deployment areas

SP 2.2-1 Manage the Deployment

SP 2.3-1 Measure Improvement Effects

Organizational Process Definition (OPD)

A Process Management process area at Maturity Level 3

Purpose

The purpose of Organizational Process Definition (OPD) is to establish and maintain a usable set of organizational process assets.

Specific Practices by Goal

SG 1 Establish Organizational Process Assets

SP 1.1-1 Establish Standard Processes

SP 1.2-1 Establish Life-Cycle Model Descriptions

SP 1.3-1 Establish Tailoring Criteria and Guidelines

SP 1.4-1 Establish the Organization's Measurement Repository

SP 1.5-1 Establish the Organization's Process Asset Library

Organizational Process Focus (OPF)

A Process Management process area at Maturity Level 3

Purpose

The purpose of Organizational Process Focus (OPF) is to plan and implement organizational process improvement based on a thorough understanding of the current strengths and weaknesses of the organization's processes and process assets.

Specific Practices by Goal

SG 1 Determine Process Improvement Opportunities

SP 1.1-1 Establish Organizational Process Needs

SP 1.2-1 Appraise the Organization's Processes

SP 1.3-1 Identify the Organization's Process Improvements

SG 2 Plan and Implement Process Improvement Activities

SP 2.1-1 Establish Process Action Plans

SP 2.2-1 Implement Process Action Plans

SP 2.3-1 Deploy Organizational Process Assets

SP 2.4-1 Incorporate Process-Related Experiences into the Organizational Process Assets

Organizational Process Performance (OPP)

A Process Management process area at Maturity Level 4

Purpose

The purpose of Organizational Process Performance (OPP) is to establish and maintain a quantitative understanding of the performance of the organization's set of standard processes in support of quality and process-performance objectives, and to provide the process performance data, baselines, and models to quantitatively manage the organization's projects.

Specific Practices by Goal

SG 1 Establish Performance Baselines and Models

SP 1.1-1 Select Processes

SP 1.2-1 Establish Process Performance Measures

SP 1.3-1 Establish Quality and Process Performance Objectives

SP 1.4-1 Establish Process Performance Baselines

SP 1.5-1 Establish Process Performance Models

Organizational Training (OT)

A Process Management process area at Maturity Level 3

Purpose

The purpose of Organizational Training (OT) is to develop the skills and knowledge of people so that they can perform their roles effectively and efficiently.

Specific Practices by Goal

SG 1 Establish an Organizational Training Capability

SP 1.1-1 Establish the Strategic Training Needs

SP 1.2-1 Determine Which Training Needs Are the Responsibility of the Organization

SP 1.3-1 Establish an Organizational Training Tactical Plan

SP 1.4-1 Establish Training Capability SG 2 Provide Necessary Training

SP 2.1-1 Deliver Training

SP 2.2-1 Establish Training Records

SP 2.3-1 Assess Training Effectiveness

Product Integration (PI)

An Engineering process area at Maturity Level 3

Purpose

The purpose of Product Integration (PI) is to assemble the product from the product components, ensure that the product, as integrated, functions properly and deliver the product.

Specific Practices by Goal

SG 1 Prepare for Product Integration

SP 1.1-1 Determine Integration Sequence

SP 1.2-1 Establish the Product Integration Environment

SP 1.3-1 Establish Product Integration Procedures and Criteria

SG 2 Ensure Interface Compatibility

SP 2.1-1 Review Interface Descriptions for Completeness

SP 2.2-1 Manage Interfaces

SG 3 Assemble Product Components and Deliver the Product

SP 3.1-1 Confirm Readiness of Product Components for Integration

SP 3.2-1 Assemble Product Components

SP 3.3-1 Evaluate Assembled Product Components

SP 3.4-1 Package and Deliver the Product or Product Component

Project Monitoring and Control (PMC)

A Project Management process area at Maturity Level 2

Purpose

The purpose of Project Monitoring and Control (PMC) is to provide an understanding of the project's progress so that appropriate corrective actions can be taken when the project's performance deviates significantly from the plan.

Specific Practices by Goals

SG 1 Monitor Project against Plan

SP 1.1-1 Monitor Project Planning Parameters

SP 1.2-1 Monitor Commitments

SP 1.3-1 Monitor Project Risks

SP 1.4-1 Monitor Data Management

SP 1.5-1 Monitor Stakeholder Involvement

SP 1.6-1 Conduct Progress Reviews

SP 1.7-1 Conduct Milestone Reviews

SG 2 Manage Corrective Action to Closure

SP 2.1-1 Analyze Issues SP 2.2-1 Take Corrective Action

SP 2.3-1 Manage Corrective Action

Project Planning (PP)

A Project Management process area at Maturity Level 2

Purpose

The purpose of Project Planning (PP) is to establish and maintain plans that define project activities.

Specific Practices by Goal

SG 1 Establish Estimates

SP 1.1-1 Estimate the Scope of the Project

SP 1.2-1 Establish Estimates of Work Product and Task Attributes

SP 1.3-1 Define Project Life Cycle

SP 1.4-1 Determine Estimates of Effort and Cost

SG 2 Develop a Project Plan

SP 2.1-1 Establish the Budget and Schedule

SP 2.2-1 Identify Project Risks

SP 2.3-1 Plan for Data Management

SP 2.4-1 Plan for Project Resources

SP 2.5-1 Plan for Needed Knowledge and Skills

SP 2.6-1 Plan Stakeholder Involvement

SP 2.7-1 Establish the Project Plan

SG 3 Obtain Commitment to the Plan

SP 3.1-1 Review Plans that Affect the Project

SP 3.2-1 Reconcile Work and Resource Levels

SP 3.3-1 Obtain Plan Commitment

Process and Product Quality Assurance (PPQA)

A Support process area at Maturity Level 2

Purpose

The purpose of Process and Product Quality Assurance (PPQA) is to provide staff and management with objective insight into processes and associated work products.

Specific Practices by Goal

SG 1 Objectively Evaluate Processes and Work Products

SP 1.1-1 Objectively Evaluate Processes

SP 1.2-1 Objectively Evaluate Work Products and Services

SG 2 Provide Objective Insight

SP 2.1-1 Communicate and Ensure Resolution of Noncompliance Issues

SP 2.2-1 Establish Records

Quantitative Project Management (QPM)

A Project Management process area at Maturity Level 4

Purpose

The purpose of the Quantitative Project Management (QPM) process area is to quantitatively manage the project's defined process to achieve the project's established quality and process-performance objectives.

Specific Practices by Goal

SG 1 Quantitatively Manage the Project

SP 1.1-1 Establish the Project's Objectives

SP 1.2-1 Compose the Defined Processes

SP 1.3-1 Select the Sub processes that Will Be Statistically Managed

SP 1.4-1 Manage Project Performance

SG 2 Statistically Manage Sub process Performance

SP 2.1-1 Select Measures and Analytic Techniques

SP 2.2-1 Apply Statistical Methods to Understand Variation

SP 2.3-1 Monitor Performance of the Selected Sub processes

SP 2.4-1 Record Statistical Management Data

Requirements Development (RD)

An Engineering process area at Maturity Level 3

Purpose

The purpose of Requirements Development (RD) is to produce and analyze customer, product, and product-component requirements.

Specific Practices by Goal

SG 1 Develop Customer Requirements

SP 1.1-1 Collect Stakeholder Needs

SP 1.1-2 Elicit Needs

SP 1.2-1 Develop the Customer Requirements

SG 2 Develop Product Requirements

SP 2.1-1 Establish Product and Product-Component Requirements

SP 2.2-1 Allocate Product-Component Requirements

SP 2.3-1 Identify Interface Requirements

SG 3 Analyze and Validate Requirements

SP 3.1-1 Establish Operational Concepts and Scenarios

SP 3.2-1 Establish a Definition of Required Functionality

SP 3.3-1 Analyze Requirements

SP 3.4-3 Analyze Requirements to Achieve Balance

SP 3.5-1 Validate Requirements

SP 3.5-2 Validate Requirements with Comprehensive Methods

Requirements Management (REQM)

An Engineering process area at Maturity Level 2

Purpose

The purpose of Requirements Management (REQM) is to manage the requirements of the project's products and product components and to identify inconsistencies between those requirements and the project's plans and work products.

Specific Practices by Goal

SG 1 Manage Requirements

SP 1.1-1 Obtain an Understanding of Requirements

SP 1.2-2 Obtain Commitment to Requirements SP 1.3-1 Manage Requirements Changes SP 1.4-2 Maintain Bidirectional Traceability of Requirements

SP 1.5-1 Identify Inconsistencies between Project Work and Requirements

Risk Management (RSKM)

A Project Management process area at Maturity Level 3

Purpose

The purpose of Risk Management (RSKM) is to identify potential problems before they occur so that risk-handling activities can be planned and invoked as needed across the life of the product or project to mitigate adverse impacts on achieving objectives.

Specific Practices by Goal

SG 1 Prepare for Risk Management

SP 1.1-1 Determine Risk Sources and Categories

SP 1.2-1 Define Risk Parameters

SP 1.3-1 Establish a Risk Management Strategy

SG 2 Identify and Analyze Risks

SP 2.1-1 Identify Risks

SP 2.2-1 Evaluate, Categorize, and Prioritize Risks

SG 3 Mitigate Risks

SP 3.1-1 Develop Risk Mitigation Plans

SP 3.2-1 Implement Risk Mitigation Plans

Supplier Agreement Management (SAM)

A Project Management process area at Maturity Level 2

Purpose

The purpose of Supplier Agreement Management (SAM) is to manage the acquisition of products from suppliers for which there exists a formal agreement.

Specific Practices by Goal

SG 1 Establish Supplier Agreements

SP 1.1-1 Determine Acquisition Type

SP 1.2-1 Select Suppliers

SP 1.3-1 Establish Supplier Agreements

SG 2 Satisfy Supplier Agreements

SP 2.1-1 Review COTS Products

SP 2.2-1 Execute the Supplier Agreement

SP 2.3-1 Accept the Acquired Product

SP 2.4-1 Transition Products

Technical Solution (TS)

An Engineering process area at Maturity Level 3

Purpose

The purpose of Technical Solution (TS) is to design, develop, and implement solutions to requirements. Solutions, designs, and implementations encompass products, product components, and product-related life-cycle processes either alone or in appropriate combination.

Specific Practices by Goal

SG 1 Select Product-Component Solutions

SP 1.1-1 Develop Alternative Solutions and Selection Criteria

SP 1.1-2 Develop Detailed Alternative Solutions and Selection Criteria

SP 1.2-2 Evolve Operational Concepts and Scenarios

SP 1.3-1 Select Product-Component Solutions

SG 2 Develop the Design

SP 2.1-1 Design the Product or Product Component

SP 2.2-3 Establish a Technical Data Package

SP 2.3-1 Establish Interface Descriptions

SP 2.3-3 Design Interfaces Using Criteria

SP 2.4-3 Perform Make, Buy, or Reuse Analyses

SG 3 Implement the Product Design

SP 3.1-1 Implement the Design

SP 3.2-1 Develop Product Support

Documentation Validation (VAL)

An Engineering process area at Maturity Level 3

Purpose

The purpose of Validation (VAL) is to demonstrate that a product or product component fulfills its intended use when placed in its intended environment.

Specific Practices by Goal

SG 1 Prepare for Validation

SP 1.1-1 Select Products for Validation

SP 1.2-2 Establish the Validation Environment

SP 1.3-3 Establish Validation Procedures and Criteria

SG 2 Validate Product or Product Components

SP 2.1-1 Perform Validation

SP 2.2-1 Analyze Validation Results

Verification (VER)

An Engineering process area at Maturity Level 3

Purpose

The purpose of Verification (VER) is to ensure that a selected work product meets their specified requirements.

Specific Practices by Goal

SG 1 Prepare for Verification

SP 1.1-1 Select Work Products for Verification

SP 1.2-2 Establish the Verification Environment

SP 1.3-3 Establish Verification Procedures and Criteria

SG 2 Perform Peer Reviews

SP 2.1-1 Prepare for Peer Reviews

SP 2.2-1 Conduct Peer Reviews

SP 2.3-2 Analyze Peer Review Data

SG 3 Verify Selected Work Products

SP 3.1-1 Perform Verification

SP 3.2-2 Analyze Verification Results and Identify Corrective Action.

7

Six Sigma

(B) What is six sigma?

Sigma is a statistical measure of variation in a process. We say a process has achieved six sigma if the quality is 3.4 DPMO (Defect per Million opportunities). It's a problem solving methodology that can be applied to a process to eliminate the root cause of defects and costs associated with the same.

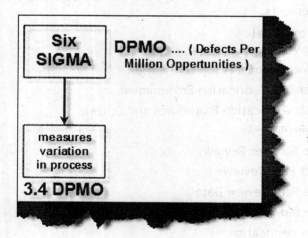

Figure: Six Sigma.

(I) Can you explain the different methodology for execution and design process in SIX sigma?

The main focus of SIX sigma is on reducing defects and variations in the processes. DMAIC and DMADV are the models used in most SIX sigma initiatives. DMADV is model for designing process while DMAIC is for improving the process.

DMADV model has the below five steps:

· **Define:** Determine the project goals and the requirements of customers (external and internal).

- **Measure:** Assess customer needs and specifications.
- **Analyze:** Examine process options to meet customer requirements.
- **Design:** Develop the process to meet the customer requirements.
- **Verify:** Check the design to ensure that it's meeting customer requirements

DMAIC model has the below five steps:

- Define the projects, the goals, and the deliverables to customers (internal and external). Describe and quantify both the defect and the expected improvement.
- Measure the current performance of the process. Validate data to make sure it is credible and set the baselines.
- Analyze and determine the root cause(s) of the defects. Narrow the causal factors to the vital few.
- Improve the process to eliminate defects. Optimize the vital few and their interrelationships.
- Control the performance of the process. Lock down the gains.

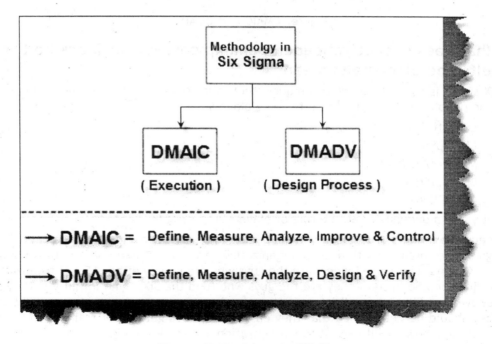

Figure: Methodology in SIX Sigma

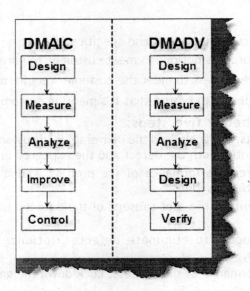

Figure: DMAIC and DMADV

(I) What does executive leaders, champions, Master Black belt, green belts and black belts mean?

SIX sigma is not only about techniques, tools and statistics, but the main thing depends upon people. In SIX sigma there five key players:

· Executive leaders
· Champions
· Master black belt
· Black belts
· Green belts

Let's try to understand all the role of players step by step.

Executive leaders: They are the main person who actually decides that we need to do SIX sigma. They promote it throughout organization and ensure commitment of the organization in SIX sigma. Executive leaders are the guys who are mainly either CEO or from the board of directors. So in short they are the guys who fund the SIX sigma initiative. They should believe that SIX sigma will improve the organization process and that they will succeed. They should be determined that they ensure resources get proper training on SIX sigma, understand how it will benefit the organization and track the metrics.

Champions: Champion is a normally a senior manager of the company. He promotes SIX sigma mainly between the business users. He understand SIX sigma thoroughly, serves as a coach and mentor, selects project, decides objectives, dedicates resource to black belts and removes obstacles which come across black belt players. Historically Champions always fight for a cause. In SIX sigma they fight to remove black belt hurdles.

Master Black-Belt: This role requires highest level of technical capability in SIX sigma. Normally organizations that are just starting up with SIX sigma will not have the same. So normally outsiders are recruited for the same. The main role of Master Black belt is to train, mentor and guide. He helps the executive leaders in selecting candidates, right project, teach the basic and train resources. They regularly meet with black belt and green belt training and mentor them.

Black-Belt: Black belt leads a team on a selected project which has to be show cased for SIX sigma. They are mainly responsible to find out variations and see how these variations can be minimized. Mast black belt basically selects a project and train resources, but black belt are the guys who actually implement it. Black belt normally works in projects as team leads or project manager. They are central to SIX sigma as they are actually implementing SIX sigma in the organization.

Green Belt: Green belt assist black belt in their functional areas. They are mainly in projects and work part time on SIX sigma implementation. They apply SIX sigma methodologies to solve problems and improve process at the bottom level. They have just enough knowledge of SIX sigma and they help to define the base of SIX sigma implementation in the organization. They assist black belt in SIX sigma implementation actually.

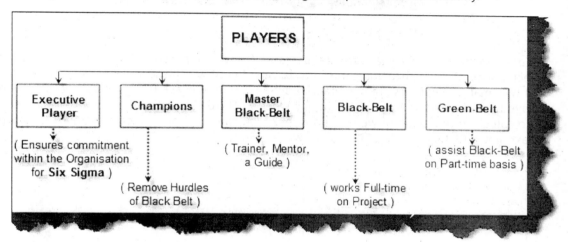

Figure: SIX key players

(I) What are the different kinds of variations used in six sigma?

Variation is the basis of six sigma. It defines how much changes are happening in an output of a process. So if a process is improved then this should reduce variations. In six sigma we identify variations in the process, control them and reduce or eliminate defects. Now let's understand how we can measure variations.

There are four basic ways of measuring variations Mean, Median, Mode and Range. Let's understand each of these variations in more depth for better analysis.

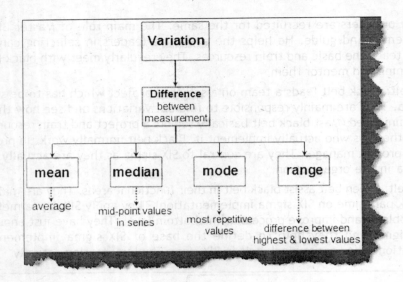

Figure: Different variations in Six sigma

Mean: In mean the variations are measured and compared using math's averaging techniques. For instance you can see the below figure which shows two weekly measures of how many computers are manufactured. So for that we have tracked two weeks one we have named as Week 1 and the other as Week 2. So to calculate variation by using mean we calculate the mean of week1 and week2. You can see from the calculations below we have got 5.083 for week and 2.85 for week2. So we have a variation of 2.23.

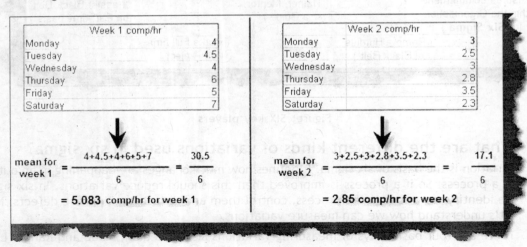

Figure: Measuring variations by using Mean

Median: Median value is a mid point in our range of data. Mid point can be found out using by finding the difference between highest and lowest value then divide it by two and finally add the lowest value to the same. For instance for the below figure in week1 we have 4 as the lowest value and 7 as the highest value. So first we subtract the lowest value from the highest value i.e. 7 -4. Then we divide it by two and add the lowest value. So for week1 the median is 5.5 and for week2 the median is 2.9. So the variation is 5.5 - 2.9.

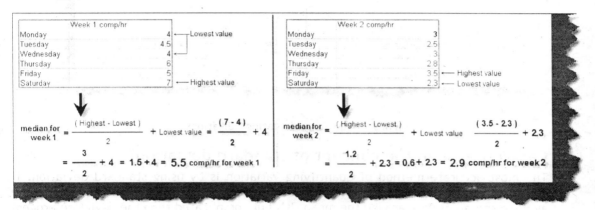

Figure: Median for calculating variations

Range: Range is nothing but spread of value for a particular data range. In short it is the difference between highest and lowest values in particular data range. For instance you can see for recorded computer data of two week we have found out the range values by subtracting the highest value from the lowest.

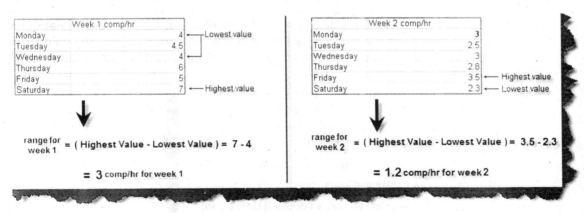

Figure: Range for calculating variations

Mode: Mode is nothing but the most occurred values in a data range. For instance in our computer manufacturing data range 4 is the most occurred value in Week1 and 3 is the most occurred value in week 2. So the variation is 1 between these data ranges.

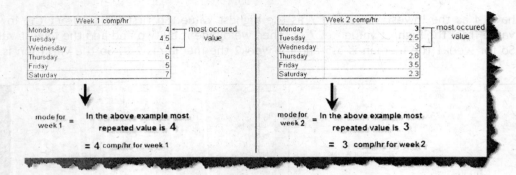

Figure: Mode for calculating variations

(A)   Can you explain the concept of standard deviation?

The most accurate method of quantifying variation is by using standard deviation. It indicates the degree of variation in a set of measurement or a process by measuring the average spread of data around the mean. It's but complicated than the deviation process discussed in the previous question, but it does give accurate information.

> *Note:*   *To understand standard deviation we will be going through a bit of maths so please co-operate and keep your head cool. In the below steps we will go step by step and understand how we can implement standard deviation.*

Below is the formula for Standard deviation. "ó" symbol stands for standard deviation. X is the observed values; X (with the top bar) is the arithmetic mean and n is the number of observations. The formulae must be looking complicated by but let is break up in to steps and understand it better.

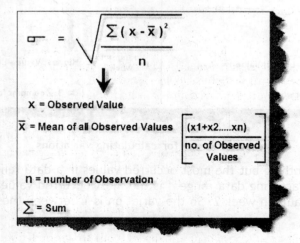

Figure: Standard deviation formulae

The first step is to calculate the mean. This can be calculated by adding all the observed values and dividing the same by the number of observed values.

Step 1 :

x = x1, x2 & x3 are Observed Values

x = 5, 2 & 4 are Observed Values

$$\text{To Calculate Mean Value } \bar{x} = \frac{x1+x2+x3}{\text{no. of Observed Values}}$$

number of Observed Values = 3 (as we have 3 value under Observation)

$$\bar{x} = \frac{5+2+4}{3} = 3.666667$$

Figure: Step 1 Standard deviation

The second step is to subtract the average from each observation, square them and then sum them. Because we square them we will not get negative values. Below figure indicates the same in very detail manner.

Step 2:

$$\text{To Calculate } \Sigma (x - \bar{x})^2 = (x1 - \bar{x})^2 + (x2 - \bar{x})^2 + (x3 - \bar{x})^2$$

$$= (5 - 3.666667)^2 + (2 - 3.666667)^2 + (4 - 3.666667)^2$$

$$= 1.777778 + 2.777778 + 0.111111$$

$$= 4.666667$$

Figure: Step 2 Standard deviation

In the third step we divide the same with the number of observations as shown the figure.

Step 3:

Now divide with the number of Observation (n) = 3

According to Formula,

$$\sigma = \sqrt{\frac{\sum (x - \bar{x})^2}{n}} = \sqrt{\frac{4.666667}{3}}$$

$$\sigma = \sqrt{1.555556}$$

Figure: Step 3 Standard deviation

In the final step we take the square root which gives the standard deviation.

Step 4:

$$\sigma = \sqrt{1.555556}$$

Now taking the Square root of the above step as follows

$$\sigma = 1.247219$$

Figure: Step 4 standard deviation

Note: *Below are some questions which we have not answered and left it as an exercise to the readers. We will definitely try to cover the same in the coming second edition.*

(B) Can you explain the concept of fish bone/ Ishikawa diagram?

There are situations where we need to analyze what caused the failure or problem in a project. Fish bone or Ishikawa diagram is one of the important concept which can help you list down your root cause of the problem. Fish bone was conceptualized by Ishikawa, so in the honor of its inventor this concept was named as Ishikawa diagram. Inputs to conduct a fish bone diagram comes from discussion and brain storming with people who were involved in the project. Below figure shows how the structure of the Ishikawa diagram is.

Below is a sample fish bone diagram. The main bone is the problem which we need to address and to know what caused the failure. For instance the below fish bone is constructed to know what caused the project failure. To know this cause we have taken four main bones as inputs Finance, Process, People and Tools. For instance on the people front there are many resignations → this was caused because there was no job satisfaction → this was caused because the project was a maintenance project. In the same way causes are analyzed on the Tools front also. In tools → No tools were used in the project → because no resource had enough knowledge about the same → this happened because of lack of planning. In process front the process was adhoc → this was because of tight dead lines → this was caused because marketing people over promised and did not negotiate properly with the end customer.

Now once the diagram is drawn the end bones of the fish bone signify the main cause of project failure. From the below diagram here's a list:

·   No training was provided for the resources regarding tool.
·   Marketing people over promised with customer which lead to tight dead lines.
·   Resources resigned because it's a maintenance project.

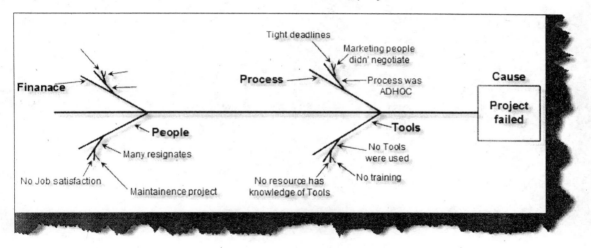

Figure: Fish bone / Ishikawa diagram

(B) What is Pareto principle?

Pareto principle also paraphrased as 80/20 principle is simple effective problem tackling way in management. It says that 20% of your problems lead to other 80 % of problems. So rather than concentrating on the 80% of problem if you concentrate on 20% of problems you can save lot of trouble. So in Pareto you analyze the problems and only concentrate on 20% of your vital problems.

If you look at the above fish bone diagram we have discussed all the root problem is due to only three reasons:

·   No tools are used.

· No process is defines.
· Many resignations.

So if we tackle these problems we can solve all the other problems.

(A) Can you explain QFD?

(A) Can you explain FMEA?

(A) Can you explain X bar charts?

(A) Can you explain Flow charting and brain storming?

The above questions are left for the second edition.

8

Agile Development

(I) What does Agile mean?

Dictionary meaning of Agile is quick moving. Now how does that apply to software? Agile development methodology considers software as the most important entity and accepts user requirement changes. Agile advocates that we should accept changes and deliver the same in small releases. Agile accepts change as a norm and encourages constant feedback from the end user.

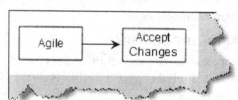

Figure: Agile

Below figure shows how Agile differs in principles from traditional methodologies.

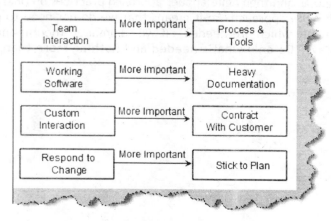

Figure: Change of Agile thinking

- It's not necessary to have hi-fi tools and process but a good team interaction can solve lot of problems.
- Working software is more important than documentation.
- Management should not pay attention to only customer contract rather interact with customer and analyze the requirements.
- In traditional methodologies we pledge to stick our plans but agile says "If the customer wants to change, analyze and change your plan accordingly".

Below are principles of Agile methodology:

- Welcome change and adapt to changing requirements
- Working software is the main measure of progress.
- Customer satisfaction is the most important thing and that can be attained by rapid, continuous delivery of useful software
- Day to day meetings between business people and development team is a must.
- Business and developers must work together. Face to face to communication is the most important thing.
- Deliver and update software regularly. In Agile we do not deliver software in one go, but rather we deliver frequently and deliver the important features first.
- Build projects around teams of motivated and trustful people.
- Design and execution should be kept simple.
- Strive for technical excellence in design and execution.
- Allow team to organize themselves.

(I)   Can you explain Agile modeling?

Agile modeling is an approach to the modeling aspects of software development. It's a practice for modeling and documentation for software systems. In one line

> *It's a collection of best practices for software modelling in light-weight manner.*

In abstraction we can say it augments other software processes. For instance let's say your company is using UML and then Agile applies approach practices on UML.For example "Keep things simple" is Agile approach. So it means that we do not need to use all diagrams in our project, use only which are needed. If we summarize then in one word we can say Agile modeling says **"Do only what's needed and nothing more than that"**.

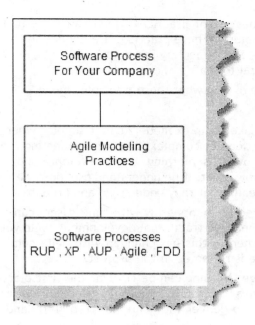

Figure: Agile Modeling

(A) What are core and supplementary principles in Agile modeling?

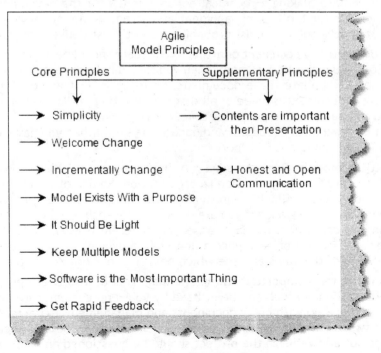

Figure: Agile Model Principles

Agile modeling defines set of practices which can show us the way towards becoming successful Agile modelers. These practices are divided in to two sections one the "Core Principles" and other "Supplementary Principles". Below figure 'Agile Model Principles' shows the same in a pictorial format.

Let's understand one by one what those principles mean.

Core Principles

Simplicity: Do not make complex model keep it simple. When you can explain your team with a pen and paper do not complex it by using modeling tool like rational rose. Do not add complexity to show off something. If the developer understands only flow chart then explain him with a flow chart, if he understand pseudo-code then use pseudo-code and so on. So look at your team what they understand and prepare document in a similar fashion.

Welcome Change: Requirements grow with time. Users can change the requirements as the project moves ahead. In traditional development cycle you will always hear the word "Freeze the requirement", this has changed with Agile coming in. In Agile we welcome change and the same is reflected in the project.

Incrementally change: Nothing can be right at the first place itself. You can categorize your development with "The most required", "Needed features" and "Luxury features". In the first phase try to deliver the "The most required" and then incrementally deliver the other features.

Model exists with a purpose: Model should exist for a purpose and not for the sake of just existing. We should know who our target audience for whom the model is made. For instance if you are making a technical documents it's for the developers, a power point presentation it's for the top management and so on. If the model does not have target audience then it should not exist probably. In short "just deliver enough and not more".

It should be light: Any document or artifact you create should be also updated over a period of time. So if you make 10 documents then you should note that as the source code changes you also need to update those documents. So make it light as possible. For instance if your technical document is made of all diagrams existing in UML, it becomes important to update all diagrams over a period of time, which is again a pain. So keep it light weight make a simple technical document and update the same when you have logical ends in the project, rather than updating it periodically.

Keep multiple models: Project issues vary from project to project and the same project behavior can vary from organization to organization. So do not think one model can solve all issues keep yourself flexible and think about multiple models. Depending on situation apply the model. For instance if you are using UML for technical documentation then every diagram in UML can reflect the same aspects in different way. For instance a class diagram shows the static view of project while a flow chart a dynamic view. So keep yourself flexible by using different diagrams and see which best fits your project or the scenario.

Software is the most important thing: The main goal of a software project is to produce high quality software which can be utilized by your end customer in a effective manner. Many projects end up with bulky documents and management artifacts. Documentation is for the software and not software for the documentation. So any document or activity which does not add value to the project should be questioned and validated.

Get Rapid and regular feedbacks: Software is finally made for the user. So try to get feedback on regular basis from the end user. Do not work in isolation involve the end user. Work closely with the end customer, get feedback, analyze requirements and try to meet there need.

Supplementary principles

Content is important than presentation: The look and feel is not important rather the content or the message to be delivered by the content is important. For instance you can represent project architecture using complex UML diagrams, simple flow chart or by using simple text. It will look fancy that you can draw complex UML diagrams but if the end developer does not understand UML then it ends no where. A simple textual explanation could have met the requirement for communicating your architecture to the end developer / programmer.

Honest and open communication: Take suggestion, be honest and keep your mind open to new model. Be frank with the top management if your project is behind schedule. An open and free environment in project keeps resources motivated and the project healthy.

(A) What is the main principle behind Agile documentation?

The main deliverable in Agile is a working software and not documentation. Documentation is a support to get the working software. In traditional delivery cycle lot of documentation where generated in design and requirement phase. But we are sure many of documentation where either created just for the sake of it or it was just created. Below are the some of the key points to make documentation Agile:

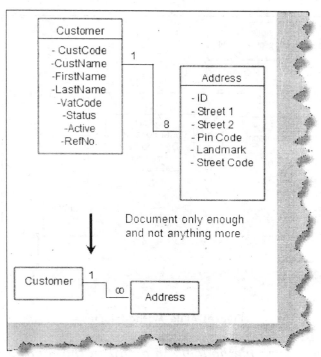

Figure: Agile documentation

Before creating any document ask a question do we need it and if we who is the stake holder. Document should exist only if needed and not for the sake of existence.

The most important thing is we need to create documentation to provide enough data and no more than that. It should be simple and should communicate to stakeholders what it needs to communicate. For instance figure 'Agile Documentation' shows two views for a simple class diagram. In the first view we have shown all the properties for "Customer" and the "Address" class. Now have a look at the second view where we have only shown the broader level view of the classes and relationships between them. The second view is enough and not more. If the developer wants to get in to details we can do that during development.

Document only for the current and not for future. In short whatever documentation we require now we should produce and not something we need in the future. Documentation changes its form as it travels through every cycle. For instance in the requirement phase it's the requirement document, in design it's the technical documentation and so on. So only think which document you want to create now and not something in the future.

(I)   What are the different methodologies to implement Agile?

Agile is a thinking approach to software development which promises to remove the issues we had with traditional waterfall methodology. In order to implement Agile practically in projects we have various methodologies. Below figure 'Agile Methodologies' shows the same in more detailed manner.

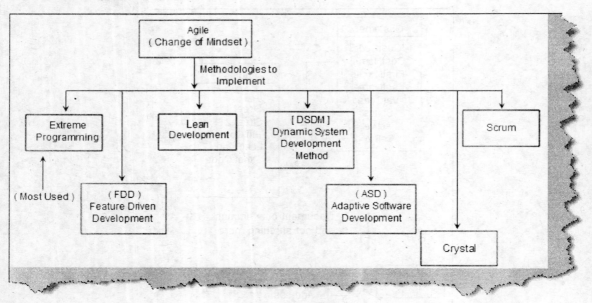

Figure: Agile Methodologies

Note: *We will cover each methodogly in detail in the coming sections.*

(l)　What is XP?

Extreme Programming (also termed as XP) is an agile software development methodology. XP focuses on coding of the software. XP has four core values and fourteen principles.

XP has four core values:

- **Communication**: Team should communicate on a regular basis, share information, discuss solutions and so on. Teams who communicate very often are able to solve problems more efficiently. For instance any kind of issues which are resolved in a cryptic fashion send an email to the whole team. This ensures that knowledge is shared with every one and in your absence some other developer can solve the problem.
- **Simplicity**: Keep things simple. Either it's from a process angle, technical angle or from a documentation point of view. An over complicated process or a technical architecture is only calling for problems.
- **Feedback**: Regular feedback from end user helps us to keep the project on track. So regular feedbacks should be enabled from end user and testing team.
- **Courage**: To bring change or to try something new, needs courage. When you try to bring change in an organization you are faced with huge resistance. Especially when your company is following traditional methodologies applying XP will always be resisted.

From the above four core values 14 principles are derived. Values give a broader level view while the 14 principles go deep in to how to implement XP.

- **Rapid feedbacks**: Developers should receive rapid feedbacks from the end user. This avoids confusion in the last minute of delivery. In water fall model feedbacks are received in late intervals. This is minimized in XP.
- **Keep it Simple**: Encourage simplicity in project design and process. For instance rather than using complex tools probably simple handwritten flowcharts on board can solve the problem.
- **Give incremental changes**: Whenever you update patches and updates, release it in small pieces. If you are updating numerous patches in one go and if there is a defect, it will be difficult to track the same.
- **Embrace Change**: Do not be rigid with the customer saying that we have already signed the requirement so we can not change the architecture. End customer or users are finally human beings so they can change as the project moves ahead....Accept it if it's logical.
- **Light Weight**: Keep documentation and process as simple as possible. Do not overdose the developer with unnecessary documentation. Developer's main work is coding and ensuring that the code is defect free, so he should be more concentrating on the code rather than documentation.
- **Deliver Quality**: Any code you deliver should be defect free. Be committed to your work and deliver defect free code.
- **Start small and grow big**: Many times the end customer wants to start with a big bang theory. He can start with a big team, wants all the functionalities at the first roll out and so on. Start with small team and the "must have" features to be delivered. As we add features and the work load increases gradually increase your team strength.
- **Play to win**: Take all steps which are needed to make a project success. Any type of deadline and commitment try to meet the same with true spirit.

- **Encourage honest communication**: Promote honest communication. If communication happens face to face then there is less leakage of requirement. Encourage end user to sit with developers and give feedbacks; this makes your project stronger.
- **Conduct testing honestly**: Test plans should not be created for the sake of creation. Test plan should prove actually that you are on track record.
- **Adapt according to situation**: No two projects are same, no two organization are same and behavior of people from person to person. So it's very essential that our approach also adapts   according to situations.
- **Metric honesty**: Do not gather metrics for the sake of gathering or showing off to external people how many metrics your project derives. Pick metrics which makes sense to your project and helps you measure your project health.
- **Accept responsibility**: Do not impose or assign people on task which they do not like. Rather question the resource once which tasks he likes and assign accordingly. This will increase productivity to a huge level and maintains your project enthusiasm high.
- **Work with people's instincts**: Normally in a project team there are highly motivated people, moderately motivated and people with less motivation. So give power to your motivated team members and encourage them.

(I)   What are User Stories in XP and how different are they from requirement?

Use story is nothing but end users requirement. What differentiates a user story from a requirement is that they are short and sweet. In one sentence they are just enough and nothing more than that. User story ideally should be written on index cards. Below figure 'User Story Index Card' shows the card. Its   3 x 5 inches (8 x 13 cm) card. This will keep your stories as small as possible. Requirement document go in pages. As we are keeping the stories short its simple to read and understand. Traditional requirement documents are verbose and they tend to loose the main requirement of the project.

> **Note:** *When I was working in a multinational company I remember first 50 pages of the requirement document having things like history, backtracking, author of the document etc. I was completely drained till I started reading the core requirement.*

Every story has a title, short description and estimation. We will come to the estimation part later.

> **Note:** *Theoretically it's good to have cards, but in real scenario you will not. We have seen in actual scenario project manager keeping stories in document and every story not more than 15 lines.*

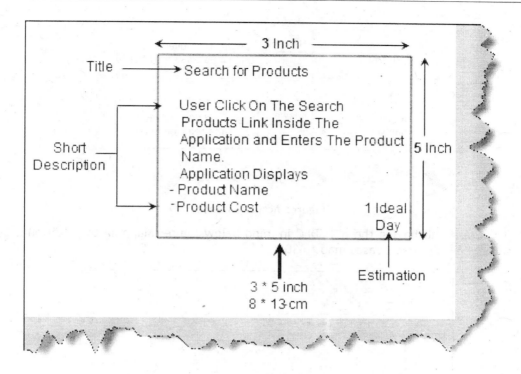

Figure: User Story Index Card

(B) Who writes User stories?

It's written and owned by the end customer and no one else.

(B) When do we say a story is valid?

Story is valid if it can be estimated.

(I) When are test plans written in XP?

Test plans are written before writing the code.

(A) Can you explain the XP development life cycle?

XP development cycle consists of two phases one is 'Release Planning' and the other is 'Iteration Planning'. In release planning we decide what should be delivered and in which priority. In iteration planning we break the requirements in to tasks and plan how to deliver those activities decided in release planning. Below figure 'Actual Essence' shows what actually these two phases deliver.

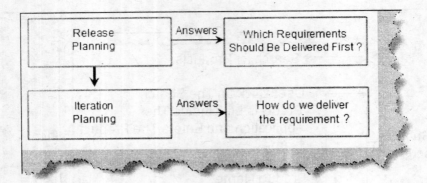

Figure: Actual Essence

If you are still having the old SDLC in mind below figure 'Mapping to Traditional Cycle' shows how the two phases map to SDLC.

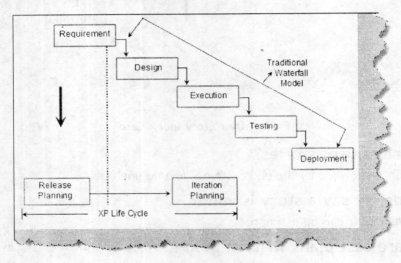

Figure: Mapping to Traditional Cycle

So let's explore both these phases in a more detailed manner. Both phases "Release Planning" and "Iteration Planning" have three common phases "Exploration", "Commitment" and "Steering".

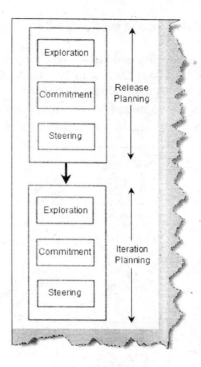

Figure: XP Planning Cycle

Release Planning

Release planning happens at the start of each project. In this phase project is broken in to small releases. Every release is broken down in to collection of user stories. Now let's try to understand the three phases in release planning.

· **Exploration**: In this phase requirement gathering is done by using user story concept (Please read the previous question on user story to understand the concept of user story). In this phase we understand the requirement to get higher level understanding. Please note only higher level. User story card is size normally 3 X 5 inch, so you can not really go detail in that size of card. We think it's absolutely fine rather than writing huge documents it sounds sense to have to the point requirement paragraphs. So here is a step by step explanation of how the exploration phase moves:

o   So the first step is user writes the story on the user card.

o   Once the story is written the developer analyzes it and determines can we estimate the user story?. If the developer can not estimate then it's again sent back to user to revise and elaborate the user story.

o   Once the user story is clear and can be estimated, ideal day or story (read about story point, ideal day and estimation in the coming questions) are calculated.

o   Now its time to say the user, ok we can not deliver everything at one go, so can you please prioritize. So in this phase the end user gives ranking to the user stories (In the next section we will deal with how a user story is ranked).

o   Once the user is done with story prioritization, its time to calculate velocity determination (In the coming section we have one complete question on velocity determination).

o   Agile is all about accepting end customer changes. In this phase we give a chance to the end user to decide if they want to change anything. If they want to change we again request the user to update the story.

o   If everything is ok we go ahead for iteration planning.

Below figure "Release planning" shows the above discussed steps in a pictorial format.

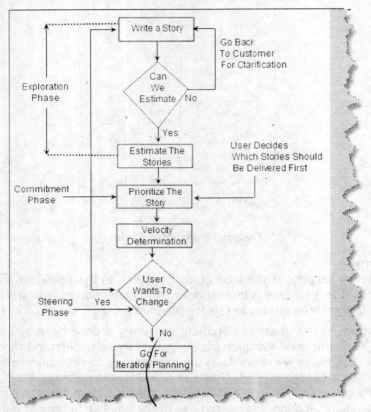

Figure: Release Planning

Iteration Planning

Iteration planning is all about going deep in to every user story and breaking the same in to tasks. This phase can also be termed as detailing of every user story. Iteration planning is all about translating the user story in to task. Below are the steps in details for iteration planning:

·   User stories which need to be delivered in this iteration are broken down in to manageable tasks.

·   Every task is then estimated. The result of the estimation is either ideal hours or task points (we will discuss about task point and ideal hours in the coming section).

·   After the tasks are estimated we need to assign the task to developers. Each programmer picks a task and own responsibility to complete the task.

·   Once he owns the responsibility he should estimate the same and commit to complete the same.

·   In XP on any development task two developers should work. In this phase the developer makes partner of his choice for developing this task.

·   In this phase we do designing of the task. We should not make lengthy and comprehensive design plans; rather it should be small and concentrated on the task. In traditional SDLC we have full devoted phase for designing and the output is a lengthy and complicated design document. One of the important characteristic of a software project is that as we come near execution we are clearer. So it's best to prepare design just before execution.

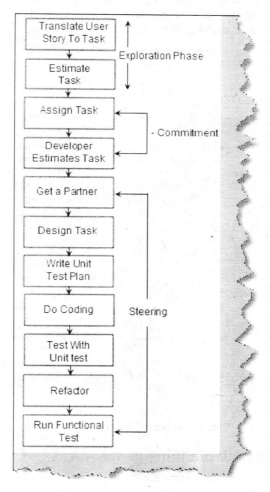

Figure: Iteration Planning

Now that you and your partner are familiar with the design plan its time to write a test plan. This is one of the huge differences as compared to original traditional SDLC.

- We first right the test plan and then start execution. Writing test plans before coding gives you a clear view of what is expected from the code.
- Once the test plan is completed its time to execute the code.
- In this phase we run the test plan and see that if all test plan pass.
- Nothing is perfect it has to be made perfect. Once you are done with coding, review the code to see if there is any scope of refactoring (Refactoring is explained in more depth in the coming sections).
- We the run the functional test to ensure everything is up to the mark.

One of the important points to realize is project is broken down in to set of releases à which is further analyzed using short user stories à user stories are further broken in to task,which is estimated and executed by the developer. Once one release is done the next release is taken for delivery. For instance the below project shown in figure 'Release, Stories and Task' has two releases one and two.

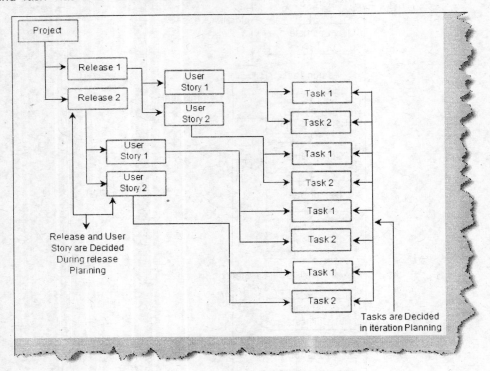

Figure: Release, Stories and Tasks

(A) Can you explain how planning game works in Extreme Programming?

The above question answers the question.

(A) How do we estimate in Agile?

If you read the Agile cycle carefully (explained in the previous section) you will see Agile estimation happens at two places.

- **User Story Level Estimation:** In this level a User story is estimated using Iteration Team velocity and the output is Ideal Man days or Story points.
- **Task Level Estimation:** This is a second level of estimation. This estimation is at the developer level according to the task assigned. This estimation ensures that the User story estimation is verified.

Estimation happens at two levels one when we take the requirement and one when we are very near to execution that's at the task level. This looks very much logical because as we are very near to complete task estimation is more and more clear. So task level estimation just comes as a cross verification for user story level estimation.

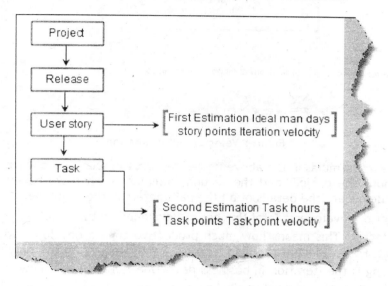

Figure: Agile Estimation

User Story Level Estimation

Estimation unit at user story in Agile is either "ideal days" or "Story points".

Ideal days are nothing but the actual time the developer spent or will spend on only coding. For instance attending phone calls, meetings, eating lunch and breakfast etc are not included in the ideal days. In old estimation technology we estimate eight hours as the complete time a developer will do coding. But actually a developer does not code continuously for eight hours, so the estimates can be very much wrong if we consider the full eight day hours.

Estimation units can also be represented in story points. **Story Points** are abstract units given to represent the size of the story. In normal scenario one story point equals to one ideal day. Story point is a relative measure. If one story is one story point and the other is two story points that means the second story will take twice the effort as compared to the first story.

Velocity determination defines how many user stories can be completed in one iteration. So first the user decides the length of the iteration. Length of iteration is decided depending on the release dates. Velocity is normally determined from history. So what ever was the last team history velocity same will be used in the further estimation. But if there is no history then the below formulae will be used:

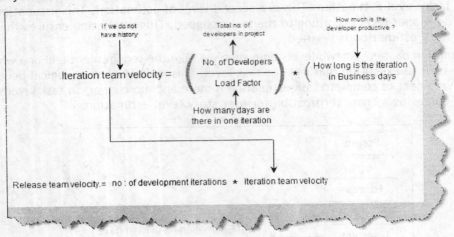

Figure: Velocity Determination

There are two formulas in the above figure the first formula is used when we do not have history about the project and the second formulae is when we have a history of the iteration. Below are the details of all the parameters in the formulae:

·   Number of developers: Total Number of developers in the iteration.
·   Load factor: This means how much productive time a developer will spend on the project. For instance if the load factor is 2 then developers are only 50% productive.
·   How long is the iteration in business days: One iteration is of how many man days.

Below figure 'Iteration and Release calculation' shows a simple sample with a team size of 5, load factor of 2, one iteration takes 11 business days and there two releases in the project.

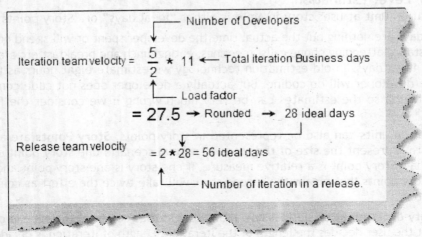

Figure: Iteration and Release calculation

Task Level Estimation

As the Agile cycle moves ahead user story is broken down in to task and assigned to each developer. Level of effort at the task level is a form of **Task points** or **Ideal hours**. Ideally one task point represents one ideal hour. Ideal hour is the time when developer spends only on coding and nothing else.

Individual Velocity determination defines how many how many ideal hours a developer has within one iteration. Below figure 'Individual Velocity Calculation' shows in detail how to get the number of ideal hours in iteration for a developer. Below is a sample calculation which shows with 8 hours a day, iteration of 11 days and load factor of 2 (i.e. developer code for only 50% time i.e. 4 hours), we get 44 ideal hours for developer in that iteration.

$$\text{Individual velocity} = \frac{(\text{ Number of Hours per day }) * (\text{ Length of Iteration in days })}{\text{Load Factor}}$$

$$= \frac{8 * 11}{2} = 44 \text{ ideal hours}$$

Figure: Individual Velocity Calculation

(A) On What basis can stories be prioritized?

User story should normally be prioritized from the business importance point of view. In real scenarios this is not the only criteria. Below are some of the factors to be accounted when prioritizing user stories:

- **Prioritize by business value**: Business user assigns a value according to the business needs. There three level of ratings for business value:
  - o **Most important features**: With out these features the software has no meaning.
  - o **Important features**: It's important to have features. But if these features do not exist there are alternatives by which user can manage.
  - o **Nice to have features**: These features are not essential features but rather it's over the top cream for the end user.
- **Prioritize by risk**: This factor helps us prioritize by risk from the development angle. Risk index is assigned from 0 to 2 and are classified in three main categories:
  - o **Completeness**
  - o **Volatility**
  - o **Complexity**

Below figure "Risk Index" shows the values and the classification accordingly.

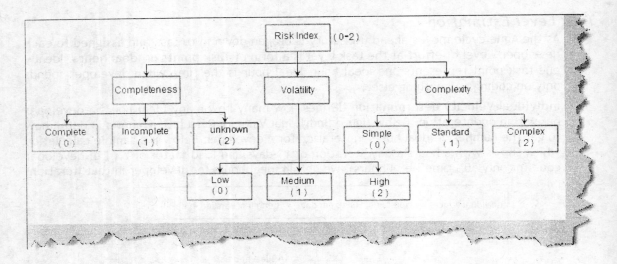

Figure: Risk Index

(A) Can you point out simple differences between Agile and traditional SDLC?

Below figure "Agile and Traditional SDLC" points out some of the main differences. If you have worked practically on both these you can point out more differences.

- Lengthy requirement documents are now simple and short user stories.

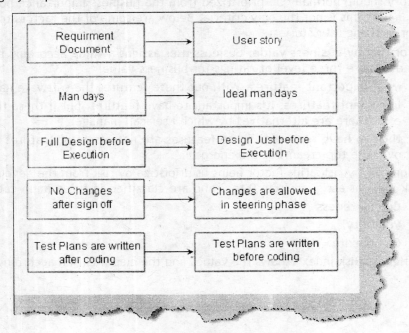

Figure: Agile and Traditional SDLC

- Estimation unit man days and man hours are now ideal days and ideal hours respectively.
- In traditional approach we freeze the requirement and complete the full design and then start coding. But in Agile we do designing task wise. So just before the developer starts a task he does design.
- In traditional SDLC we used always hear this voice 'After signoff nothing can be changed', in Agile we work for the customer, so we do accept changes.
- Unit test plans are written after coding or during coding in traditional SDLC. In Agile we write unit test plans before writing the code.

(I) Can you explain the concept of refactoring?

If you read the XP life cycle one of the things after we implement the task is code refactoring. Refactoring the process of changing the software in such a way that it does not change the behavior of the code but on the other hand improves the internal structure. No code can be perfect with architecture, coding conventions, high reusability at the first level itself. Normally it improves over the time. It helps developers to implement the necessary solution today and improve / make the code better tomorrow. Refactoring is the process of changing the system to improve the internal structure with out changing what the system does. Below are three major activities performed during refactoring:

Simplify complex code.

XP is all about light-weight and simplicity. This holds true not only for a process but also for coding. When you see a code can be simplified, discuss the same with your pair developer and implement the same. For instance below is code which was further simplified in to one equation.

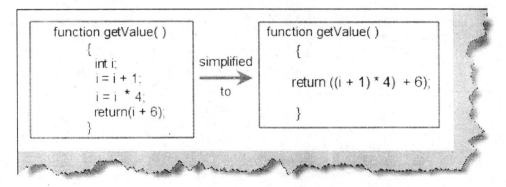

Figure: Simplify Code

Move similar operations in to reusable code.

If we are having similar operations move them to one reusable code. For instance in the below class we have various sort function which sorts by phone, code, name and date. We can combine the same in to one function called as sort and make it simple.

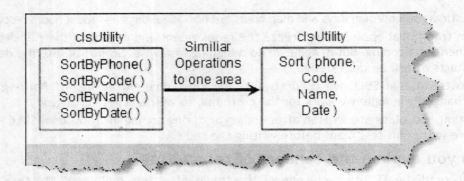

Figure: Reusable code

Remove duplications and redundancy.

When a project has constrained time lines it's very much possible that project can have lot of duplications. So when developers have executed the task they can review for these kinds of duplications. For example the below figure 'Remove duplication' shows how the phone number duplication is removed from the customer table. The customer table had repetitive fields like mobile number, land line and office number. In abstract terms these represent telephone numbers. So we split the customer table in to two tables one is the customer table and the other is customerphone and built a relationship between them.

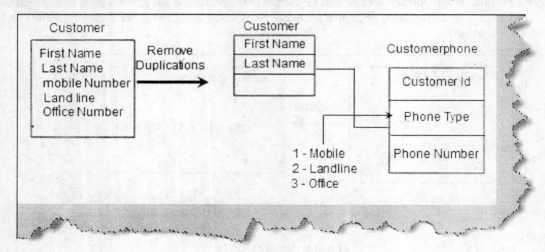

Figure: Remove Duplication

Below is again one more scenario where we have an invoice class which has two methods ("GenerateInvNo" and "CreateInvNo") and they do the same thing, generate unique invoice numbers. We can refactor / improve the code by combining these two methods in to one.

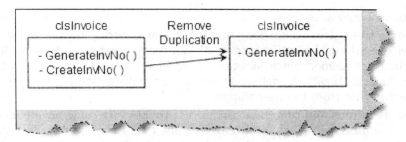

Figure: Code Duplication

> *No Code is perfect it has to be made perfect*

(B)   What is a feature in Feature Driven Development?

Feature is a process which adds value to the end customer and it can be planned. In short it has two characteristics:

·   We can plan and schedule a feature.

·   It should be something that delivers value to the end user.

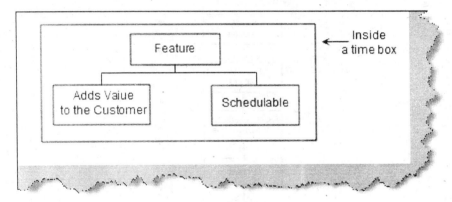

Figure: Feature

In short it's not necessary that a feature maps with use case or a user story. It should also be planned and manageable. Feature are delivered in a given time box (we will discuss this in detail in the coming sections).

(B)   Can you explain the overall structure of FDD project?

FDD is an iterative methodology to deliver projects. Rather than delivering projects in one go manner we deliver the features with in time limits. So let's understand how the FDD cycle moves. We will have two views one is the over all flow and one is the detail iteration flow.

Below figure 'Structure of FDD project' shows step by step approach for FDD project.

·   **Identify the features**: In this phase we identify the features in the project. Keep one thing in mind features are not simple user point of view requirements; we should be able to schedule a feature.

- **Prioritize the features**: Big bang theory thinking is bad. Many project managers think deliver everything at the first step itself, but that's practically difficult. Rather deliver first the most needed functionalities, then needed and then so called as over the top cream functionalities. To deliver in feature by feature manner we need to prioritize the feature list from the user's angle.

- **Define iterations and time boxes**: The first thing which must have clicked your mind is we should deliver in group of features, but that's not the case in FDD. We deliver according to the size of iteration. Iteration is based on "timeboxes" so that we know how long iteration is. Depending on the timeboxes the features can be delivered or not is decided.

The below points are looped for every iteration (below sections are covered in more detail in the coming up section).

- **Plan Iteration**: At the start of every iteration we need to plan it out, how we are going to execute the plan.

- **Create release**: We code, test and deliver according to the plan chalked out in "Plan Iteration" phase.

If everything is ok we move ahead if not we take the next iteration.

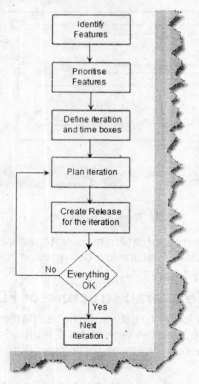

Figure: Structure of a FDD project

The above defined FDD cycle is an overall view. Let's go deep in to how every iteration will be executed. Below figure 'Steps in Iteration' shows how an iteration execution happens in a detailed manner.

· Iteration Kick Start: The length of iteration is already defined but just in case you want to validate it, then this is the phase.

· Plan features for the iteration: This is the phase where we prepare our WBS. We map the features to work packages in WBS. This plan has to be accepted by the end user.

· Study requirements: In this section we write detailed requirement document / user story or use cases.

· Design Architecture: This is the phase where we chalk out the overall architecture of the iteration and features.Once the design is done we review the architecture any issues we iterate to close the review.

· Write test plan: Before we start coding we write test plans to validate the features of the iteration.

· Execution: We do the coding according to the design decided in the design phase of the iteration.

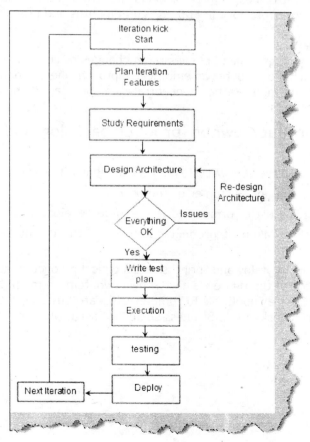

Figure: Steps in a Iteration

- Testing: Once the execution is done we run the test plans written in the 'Write test plan' phase. In case of any failures we move back to execution and fix the same. We also run the acceptance test plans from the user angle at this phase.
- Deploy: Finally we are done and we deploy the same at the end customer premises.
- Next Iteration: In this phase we analyze what features we have delivered and if not we pass it on to the next iteration. If everything is fine we take up the next iteration.

Testing is done at end of each iteration. This ensures frequent checks on each deliverable of every iteration.

(B) Can you explain the concept of time boxing?

Every iteration in FDD has to be limited to some kind of timelines. Deciding the length of timelines for every iteration is termed as time boxing. Same has been explained the previous question in a detailed manner.

(B) When to choose FDD and when to choose XP?

Iteration in XP is small i.e. between 1 to 4 weeks. This iteration sounds good for smaller projects, but when it comes to large projects, iteration go in months. That's where FDD comes under picture. Iterations in FDD can go in months and probably years.

(I) What is SCRUM?

SCRUM is a methodology which believes rapid changes of customer can not be solved by traditional approach. So it adopts an empirical approach where it believes problem can not be understood or defined. Rather concentrate on the team's ability to respond to the emerging requirements.

(I) What does product owner, product back log and sprint mean in SCRUM?

Before we understand the SCRUM cycle let's get familiar with some terms regarding SCRUM.

Product Owner is the end customer or the user.

Product back log is a list of prioritized items to be developed for a software project.

Sprint is the task breakup of product catalog. It's the detail task break down for a development team.

Below figure 'Product Catalog and Sprint' shows a typical product catalog broken in to sprint. In the left hand side of the figure we have shown two items in the product back log "Create Customer" and "Create Supplier". To complete "Create Customer" the developer need to the following sprint task "Code Business Logic", "Design UI" and "Prepare Test Plans".

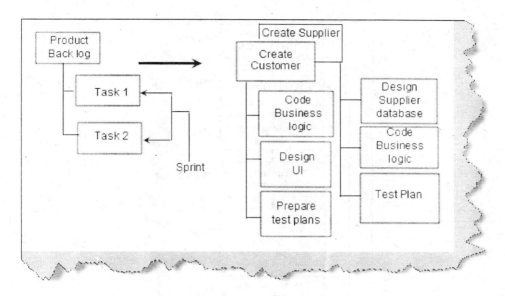

Figure: Product Catalog and Sprint

(I)   Can you explain how SCRUM flows?

Below figure 'SCRUM Flow' shows how the development flow moves in a project. We will understand the SCRUM flow step by step.

Step 1: Product owner (i.e. the customer) creates a list of product log (list of functionalities).

Step 2 and 3: In these phases we sit with the customer and prioritize the product catalog. We discuss with the customer which functionality is must and must be delivered first.

Step 4 and 5: In both these phases we breakdown the product catalog in to tasks called as sprint backlog.

Step 6: We start executing the sprint task and monitoring the sprint activity.

Step 7 and 8: Once we are done with the sprint activity, we take the next sprint / task by again going to the sprint phase.

Step 9: If there are no more sprint / task the product log is completed, which means the project is completed.

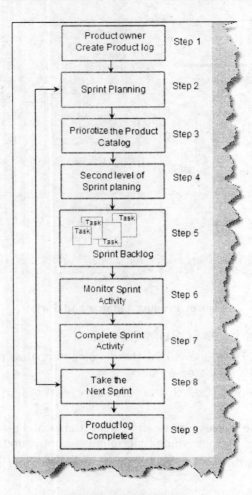

Figure: SCRUM Flow

(l) Can you explain different roles in SCRUM?

SCRUM has some different terminologies when it comes to role names in SCRUM. Below is the list of roles with what actually they mean.

People with **pig roles** are those people who are committed to the project. If the project fails it affects these people. So of the pig roles are developer, customer, project manager etc.

Product owner means the end customer or user.

Scrum master is the process driver. These are the people who drive the scrum process. They are consultants for Scrum process.

People with **chicken roles** work indirectly on the project. They do not really benefit from the project but their feedback is valuable to the project. They can not be held responsible if the project is not successful.

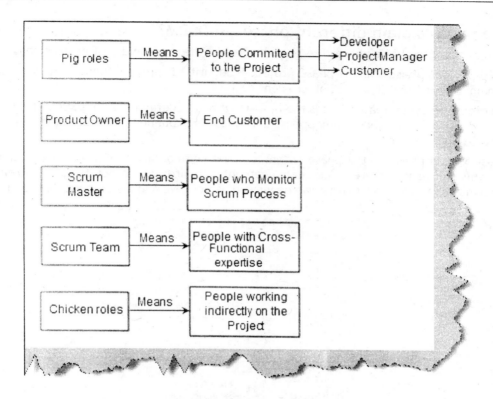

Figure: SCRUM Roles

(B) Can you explain DSDM?

DSDM also termed as Dynamic Systems Development Method has the following characteristics:

- It's based upon RAD (Rapid Application Development).
- DSDM is best suited for projects which have tight schedule and budgets.
- It's iterative and incremental.

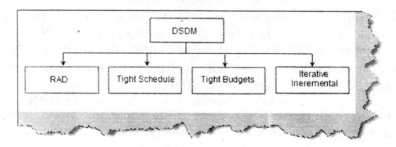

Figure: DSDM Characteristics

(I) Can you explain different phases in DSDM?

DSDM has three basic phases Pre-project, Project life cycle and Post project phase.

Pre-project phase: In this phase project is identified, project funds are allocated and commitment from all stake holder is ensured.

Project life cycle phase: This is the most lengthy and detail phase in DSDM. This is where all actual project execution happens. This phase is explained in a more detail manner in the coming section.

Post project phase: In this phase system is operating smoothly. The main activity conducted in this phase is maintenance, enhancement and project defect fixes. Maintenance, enhancement and defect fixing can be viewed as iterative and incremental nature of DSDM.

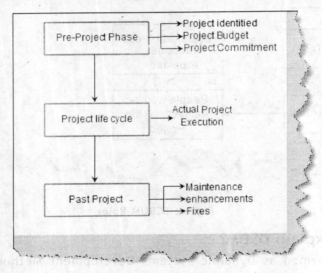

Figure: DSDM Phases

(I) Can you explain in detail project life cycle phase in DSDM?

There are in all five phases in DSDM project life cycle:

Feasibility Study: During this stage the can the project be used for DSDM is examined. For that we need to answer questions like "Can this project fulfill business needs?", "Is the project fit for DSDM?" and "What are the prime risks involved in the project?".

Business Study: Once we have concluded that the project has passed the feasibility study in this phase we do a business study. Business study involves meeting with the end customer/user to discuss about a proposed system. In one sentence it's a requirement gathering phase. Requirements are then prioritized and time boxed. So the output of this phase is a prioritized requirement list with time frames.

Functional Model Iteration: In this phase we develop prototype which is reviewed by the end user.

Design and Build Iteration: The prototype which was agreed by the user in the previous stage is designed and built in this stage and given to the end user for testing.

Implementation: Once the end user has confirmed everything is alright its time to implement the same to the end user.

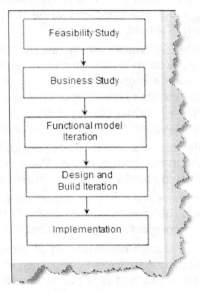

Figure: DSDM Project Life Cycle

(I)   Can you explain LSD?

Lean software development has derived its principles from lean manufacturing.

Below figure 'Principles of LSD' shows all the principles.

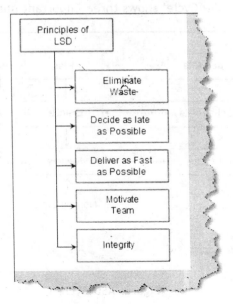

Figure: Principles of LSD

Let's understand in brief about the principles.

Eliminate waste: Only deliver what's needed to the end user. Anything more than that is a waste. In short anything which does not add value is a waste. In short we can by pass tasks and still deliver then it should be bypassed.

Decide as late as possible: Software systems are complex. The more they are near to execution more is the clarity. So delay decisions so that they can be based in facts rather than assumptions. For instance your team decides to use automation testing, but when you complete execution you come to know changes are delivered every day by the developer. After execution you conclude manual testing is the best option. Bad part will be if you have already bought an automation tool, its waste of money.

Deliver as fast as possible: faster a product is delivered, faster you will get user response and faster you can improve in the next iteration. The concept is not fast coding, but try to deliver is small user identified chunks for better understanding.

Motivate team: Team members are the most important aspect for success of any project. Motivate them, given them roles; keep your team spirit high and whatever you can do to make them feel good in the project. A highly motivated team delivers project on time.

Integrity: Software system should be delivered in loosely coupled components. Every component or module can function individually and when integrated with the project it works perfectly well. It should be a plug and play from the end user point of view. This spirit is derived from how actual production system work. You can assemble a car with wheels from one organization and seats from other organization.

(I)   Can you explain ASD?

ASD (Adaptive Software Development) accepts that change is a truth. It also accepts in principles that mistakes can happen and it's important to learn from those mistakes in the future. Below figure 'ASD Cycle' shows three important phases in ASD.

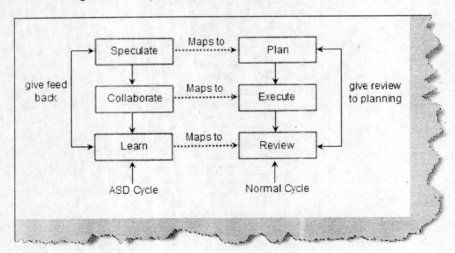

Figure: ASD Cycle

Let's understand all the three phases in a detail manner.

Speculate (nothing but planning): This is the planning phase of ASD cycle. Below figure 'Speculate' shows in detail what happens in this phase.

Define Project Scope: This is the first phase in the main speculate phase. In this we set the main goals and what's the scope of the entire project.

Set Time for Scope: Timelines are decided for the scope identified in the previous phase.

Decide the number of iterations: Depending on the time lines and the scope we identify how many iterations will the project have.

Break Scope to tasks: In this section we break the scope in to tasks. Tasks are nothing but development activity which a developer has to do to complete the scope.

Assign task to developers: Assign those task to developer.

Now that we know who will do what task, its time for coding / execution.

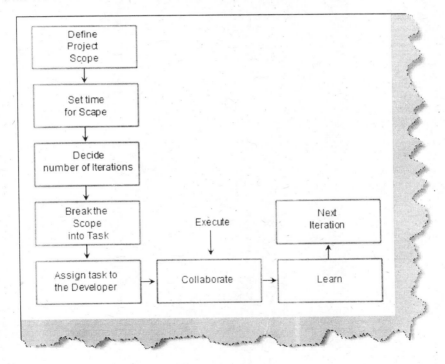

Figure: Speculate

Collaborate (coding / execution):Execute as per the task and test it.

Learn (Review and give feedback to planning): At the end of iteration see what lessons we have learnt and apply the same for the next iteration.

> **Note:** *From all the methodologies shown above, XP is the most used for Agile. One of the important points to be noted about all the XP methodologies described above is that every body believes in accepting change. Principles of all the agile methodologies are more or less same. So do not get confused just understand what every methodology concentrates on. For instance FDD plans around features, Scrum uses product owner and catalog for describing a project, DSDM gives importance to RAD. So understand the main theme of the methodologies but yes the common acceptance is every one believes on 'Accepting Changes'.*